Popular Complete Smart Series

Complete
EnglishSmart®

Revised and Updated!

Grammar

Comprehension

Vocabulary

Writing

Usage

Grade 4

Credits

Photo (Cover "children"/123RF.com)

ISBN: 978-1-897457-04-7

Complete EnglishSmart Contents

ISBN: 978-1-897457-04-7

ISBN: 978-1-897457-04-7

ISBN: 978-1-897457-04-7

ISBN: 978-1-897457-04-7

Animal Adaptation

Did you know that even in the driest deserts, coldest tundra, and darkest ocean waters live animals, plants, and organisms that are able to survive? They are able to <u>survive</u> and live to reproduce in their <u>harsh</u> environments through adaptation.

Adaptation is an evolutionary change that has developed over many generations to help animals and organisms live successfully in their habitats. The adaptations can be divided into structural and behavioural adaptations.

Camouflage, a structural adaptation, allows animals to blend in with their surroundings. For example, Arctic hares have grey or brown coats in the summer and white coats in the winter months. It helps them camouflage and <u>escape</u> from their predators. The striped tiger, a <u>formidable</u> predator, blends well in the long, tall orange-yellow grasses while <u>stalking</u> its prey.

Behavioural adaptation is the way an animal responds to and interacts with its <u>external</u> environment. In North America, raccoons have changed their habits due to land development that has destroyed their natural <u>habitats</u>. They have learned to use attics, basements, and storage sheds as homes. They <u>raid</u> and open garbage cans with their <u>dexterous</u> fingers for leftovers instead of <u>foraging</u> for food in the forests. They are fast becoming more than just a nuisance!

ISBN: 978-1-897457-04-7

Recalling Facts

A. Place "T" for true statements or "F" for false ones.

1. Adaptations help animals survive in harsh environments. _____

2. There are two types of adaptations: structural and behavioural. _____

3. Camouflage is a behavioural adaptation. _____

4. Arctic hares have white coats in the summer. _____

5. In North America, the natural habitats of raccoons have been destroyed due to land development. _____

6. Raccoons rummage through garbage cans for leftovers. _____

Using Information

B. Answer the following questions.

1. Which sentence tells us that adaptation is a lengthy process?

_____

_____

2. Why do you think Arctic hares' coats turn white in the winter?

_____

_____

3. Why do tigers need camouflage?

_____

_____

4. Why do raccoons use attics and storage sheds as homes?

_____

_____

ISBN: 978-1-897457-04-7

Nouns

- A **Noun** is a word that represents a person, a place, or a thing.
  Examples: 1. Judy, Mr. White, girl, teacher – are "person" nouns
  2. home, school, CN Tower, Canadian National Exhibition – are "place" nouns
  3. dog, bicycle, comb, radio – are "thing" nouns

C. Cross out the word in each list that is not a noun.

1. car, Susan, cried, museum

2. England, Rome, tired, carpenter

3. find, clothing, hat, purse

4. tears, years, fears, hears

5. behave, behaviour, student, test

6. walked, bookends, textbook, walkway

7. delicious, cake, cookies, pie

8. Atlantic Ocean, ran, teacher, parents

Common and Proper Nouns

- A **Proper Noun** is a specific person, place, or thing. It begins with a capital letter.
  Examples: John, Chicago, Air Canada Centre, Maple Avenue Public School

- A **Common Noun** is a person, place, or thing that is part of a classification.
  Examples: boy, city, arena, school – these are the general terms for the proper nouns above

D. Write the common nouns for the proper nouns.

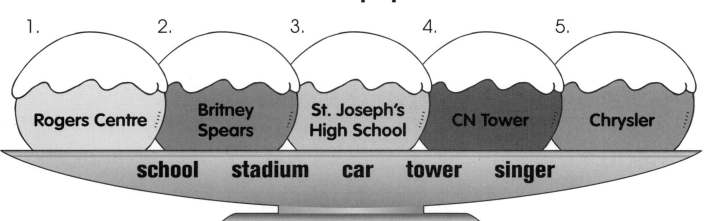

1. Rogers Centre   2. Britney Spears   3. St. Joseph's High School   4. CN Tower   5. Chrysler

school   stadium   car   tower   singer

ISBN: 978-1-897457-04-7

Words in Context

- When we are trying to understand the meaning of a word that is new to us, it is helpful to read the word in its context. **Context** is the use of the word in a sentence that reveals its meaning.

E. Match the words in Column A with the definitions in Column B.

Column A		Column B	
1. survive	_____	A.	skilful
2. harsh	_____	B.	homes
3. escape	_____	C.	severe
4. formidable	_____	D.	look for
5. stalking	_____	E.	live
6. external	_____	F.	searching
7. habitats	_____	G.	frightening
8. raid	_____	H.	outside
9. dexterous	_____	I.	following
10. foraging	_____	J.	get away

In the reading passage, there are 10 underlined words. Read the sentence in which each word appears and figure out its meaning.

F. Use any five words from Column A to write a sentence of your own.

1. _____

2. _____

3. _____

4. _____

5. _____

ISBN: 978-1-897457-04-7

The heart is a powerful <u>involuntary</u> muscle that sends blood throughout our body. We cannot control what it does. It sends a single drop of blood around the 100,000 kilometres of blood vessels about a thousand times a day. This is an <u>incredible</u> feat for a muscle that is the size of a human fist.

The Human HEART

The heart is made up of four <u>chambers</u> – two at the top and two at the bottom. At the top, the left atrium and the right atrium collect the blood and the bottom two chambers, the ventricles, pump the blood out of the heart. It takes one single heartbeat for the blood to go from the heart to the lungs where it loads up on oxygen, return to the heart, and then circulate all over the body.

To ensure that the blood travels smoothly and <u>consistently</u>, the heart uses <u>valves</u> that open and shut with the flow of blood. The valves only open one way making sure that blood does not re-enter the chambers.

When you are ready for physical action such as running, your heart speeds up and delivers large amounts of oxygen to your legs <u>enabling</u> you to run quickly. After exercising, you may feel <u>exhausted</u> as your oxygen reserve may be used up. In a few moments, however, you will recover the oxygen needed at rest and your heart will slow down and <u>resume</u> a normal rate. The <u>typical</u> heart rate of an adult is 60 – 80 beats per minute while a younger heart would beat at a rate of 80 –100 beats per minute.

ISBN: 978-1-897457-04-7

Recalling Details

A. Circle the letters of the correct answers.

1. The job of the heart is to
   A. send blood to the lungs.
   B. fill blood with oxygen.
   C. help us run quickly.
   D. send blood throughout the body.

2. The size of the human heart is about
   A. the same size as our head.
   B. the size of a fist.
   C. the size of a baseball.
   D. 5 cm in height and 2 cm in width.

3. To make sure that blood circulates smoothly, the heart uses
   A. a pacemaker.
   B. blood vessels.
   C. valves that open and shut.
   D. oxygen.

4. The valves control
   A. heartbeat.
   B. the amount of blood flow.
   C. the direction of blood flow.
   D. the amount of oxygen in the blood.

5. When you are ready for physical action, your heart delivers
   A. oxygen to your muscles.
   B. electricity to your lungs.
   C. blood to your feet.
   D. air to your lungs.

Matching the Facts

B. Match the facts.

1. ventricles _____
2. 60 – 80 beats _____
3. 4 chambers _____
4. heart _____
5. 80 – 100 beats _____
6. open one way only _____

A. adult's heart rate

B. the atriums and the ventricles

C. involuntary muscle

D. the valves to prevent re-entry of blood

E. pump blood out of the heart

F. child's heart rate

ISBN: 978-1-897457-04-7

 **Verbs**

- A **Verb** tells what the subject is doing (action) or describes the state of the noun (non-action).

  Examples (action): walk, run, jump, fly, sing, dance, scream
  Examples (non-action): am, is, are, was, were

C. Underline the verb in each sentence. Write "A" for action word or "N" for non-action word.

1. The birds flew high above the trees.   _____

2. The children played in the park.   _____

3. He is nine years old.   _____

4. Where were you last night?   _____

5. What time is it?   _____

6. The girls sang in the choir.   _____

7. He was the first to arrive.   _____

8. Do not cross the street without looking both ways.   _____

D. Fill in the blanks with the appropriate verbs provided.

| sailed | built | took | went |
| stayed | flew | camped | |

During the summer holidays, many students 1._____ on vacation. John 2._____ to England to visit his relatives. Susan 3._____ her uncle's boat. Paul 4._____ in the woods with his parents and 5._____ a campfire every night. Some students 6._____ home. They 7._____ day trips to various places.

ISBN: 978-1-897457-04-7

Crossword Puzzle

E. Use the clues to complete the crossword puzzle. The words are underlined in the reading passage.

Check the meanings of these words in context.

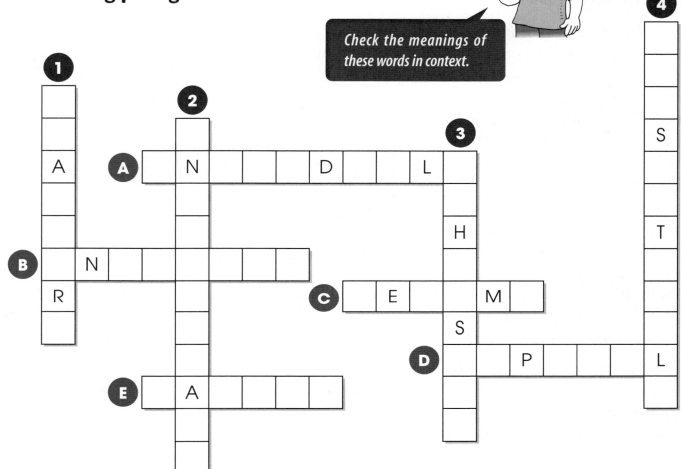

ACROSS
A. unbelievable
B. giving it the power
C. continue
D. usual
E. parts of the heart that open and shut

DOWN
1. rooms to store blood
2. acts on its own
3. tired
4. regularly, always the same

ISBN: 978-1-897457-04-7

In December, 1967, in Groote Schuur Hospital in Capetown, South Africa, medical history was made. Dr. Christian Barnard performed the first successful transplant of a human heart. The patient, Louis Washkansky, received the heart of a young woman killed in a car accident.

The transplant itself was traumatic, and so were the hours immediately after the operation. There were two main concerns: the problem of possible infection and the possibility that Mr. Washkansky's body would reject the new heart. To avoid rejection, doctors gave Mr. Washkansky drugs to lessen his body's natural defence so that rejection was less likely. However, with defence weakened, the chance for infection increased. As a precaution, the doctors made sure that everything near Mr. Washkansky was sterilized or disinfected.

The First Heart Transplant

The transplant was going very well for the first two weeks. Suddenly a dark spot appeared on one of Mr. Washkansky's lungs. Dr. Barnard and his staff did everything possible to save Mr. Washkansky, but on the nineteenth day after the operation, he died.

Although Mr. Washkansky did not survive the transplant, the operation was considered a success. It paved the way for many more attempts to follow. Today, heart transplants are performed regularly. Many of those who were born with congenital heart conditions and doomed to die at an early age now live long and healthy lives, thanks to the pioneering efforts of Dr. Christian Barnard.

ISBN: 978-1-897457-04-7

Fact or Opinion

- A **Fact** refers to information that is given in the passage. An **Opinion** is your interpretation of the information.

A. For each statement below, write "F" for fact or "O" for opinion.

1. A heart transplant is a delicate operation. _____

2. The first transplant made medical history. _____

3. The transplanted heart came from a car accident victim. _____

4. Everyone was worried about the time after the operation. _____

5. The possibility of infection was a major concern. _____

6. Rejection of the new heart was a possibility. _____

7. The drugs given to Mr. Washkansky were risky. _____

8. Everything around Mr. Washkansky had to be sterilized. _____

9. Mr. Washkansky died on the nineteenth day after the operation. _____

10. It is much safer to have a heart transplant today. _____

11. Congenital heart problems are serious. _____

12. Dr. Barnard was a hero. _____

Your Opinion

B. Write a response to the question giving your point of view.

Was Dr. Barnard a hero in the medical community? Give reasons.

_____

_____

ISBN: 978-1-897457-04-7

Adjectives and Adverbs

- We use **Adjectives** to describe nouns and **Adverbs** to describe verbs.

  The underlined words are all adjectives describing the nouns that follow them:
  the <u>little</u> boy, the <u>scary</u> story, the <u>tall</u> building, the <u>slippery</u> steps

  The underlined words are all adverbs describing the verbs next to them:
  ran <u>slowly</u>, jumped <u>high</u>, spoke <u>clearly</u>, laughed <u>hysterically</u>

C. **Underline the adjectives in the sentences. The number following each sentence tells you how many adjectives to find.**

The subject word in a sentence is not always the only noun. Remember – a noun is any person, place, or thing.

1. The excited children make for a loud party. (2)

2. The tall, husky man lifted the heavy furniture. (3)

3. The shiny new red bicycle was the perfect birthday gift. (5)

4. When the tired boy arrived home, he jumped into his warm bed. (2)

5. The expensive watch was found in the top drawer of the antique dresser. (3)

D. **Underline the adverbs in the sentences. The number following each sentence tells you how many adverbs to find.**

Adverbs often end in "ly" and they answer the questions "how", "where", "how often", and "when".

1. He had never seen such a sight. (1)

2. He moved silently and quickly like a cat. (2)

3. The athlete competed gallantly for the championship. (1)

4. The horse leaped proudly and brilliantly over the pond. (2)

5. She played bravely and courageously but lost the competition. (2)

ISBN: 978-1-897457-04-7

Words Often Confused

E. Below are groups of words that are often confused because they look alike or sound similar. Circle the words that match the meanings.

Use a dictionary to check the meanings and avoid confusion.

its	it's
clothes	cloths
here	hear
diary	dairy
feet	feat
forth	fourth
duel	dual
whether	weather
dessert	desert
loose	lose

1. belongs to it
2. material
3. a place
4. buy milk there
5. an accomplishment
6. place in a race
7. two of them
8. condition outside
9. pie or cake
10. doesn't fit

F. Use the following words to make sentences to show their meanings.

1. diary   – _____

2. whether – _____

3. desert – _____

4. forth   – _____

5. lose   – _____

ISBN: 978-1-897457-04-7

The *Incredible* Butterfly

Butterflies are among nature's most beautiful creations. While their colours have always been admired, particularly by artists, they serve other purposes. Some butterflies use their colour for camouflage. They are able to blend in with tree branches or flowers that they feed on. Some butterflies use their bright colouring as a warning to predators. The Magnificent Owl butterfly has a large dot on its wing that looks exactly like an owl's eye. This tricks predators into thinking that the butterfly is a larger animal.

Most butterflies feed on the nectar of plants. They use a long mouth part called a proboscis to dip into the flowers and suck up the nectar. Some butterflies prefer to feed on rotting fruit. Butterflies are important to nature because they pollinate plants when they feed.

During its life cycle, a butterfly goes through many changes in both body form and colour. There are four stages of butterfly life: egg, caterpillar (larva), chrysalis (pupa), and adult. After about two weeks, baby caterpillars hatch from eggs and start feeding. This stage lasts anywhere from 3 to 12 weeks, depending on the species. The pupa stage is where the caterpillar changes into a butterfly. This transformation takes about two weeks.

Butterflies are found all over the world, but the widest diversity of the species is found in tropical climates. The most familiar butterfly to North Americans is the Monarch butterfly.

ISBN: 978-1-897457-04-7

Using Information

A. Answer the following questions.

1. Why do artists in particular like butterflies?

    _____

2. How are butterflies important to nature?

    _____

3. How do butterflies defend themselves against predators?

    _____

    _____

B. State the four life cycle changes of the butterfly in order.

(adult) (egg) (pupa) (larva)

1. _____   2. _____   3. _____   4. _____

 Further Facts

C. Fill in the blanks with the words provided.

world	Magnificent Owl	flowers	pupa
nectar	Monarch	proboscis	

Butterflies feed on the 1._____ of plants. They are equipped with a 2._____ which dips into the 3._____ to get food. Caterpillars become butterflies in the 4._____ stage. Butterflies are found all over the 5._____ . The 6._____ butterfly has a large dot on its wing. The 7._____ butterfly is most familiar to North Americans.

ISBN: 978-1-897457-04-7

Pronouns

- A **Pronoun** is used in place of a noun. It must agree in gender (male or female) and number with the word it is replacing.

   Singular Pronouns:

   I   me   mine   she   her   hers   he   him   his   you   yours   it   its

   Plural Pronouns:

   we   us   ours   you   yours   they   them   theirs

D.   Write the appropriate pronouns to replace the underlined nouns.

1.   I drew <u>Sharon</u> a <u>birthday card</u>. _____ said _____ looked cute.

2.   <u>I</u> bought this book yesterday. It is _____ .

3.   Gregory called on <u>John</u> and asked if _____ could play.

4.   The <u>children</u> washed their hands before _____ had lunch.

5.   We let <u>them</u> use our car because _____ broke down.

6.   We bought tickets for the <u>show</u> early. We didn't want to miss _____ .

7.   When the new <u>students</u> arrived, the teacher asked us to help _____ .

Interrogative Pronouns

- **Interrogative Pronouns** ask questions.
   Examples: "who", "what", "whom", "which", and "whose"

E.   Place the appropriate interrogative pronoun in each space provided.

1.   _____ of the cars is the most expensive?

2.   _____ will be joining us for dinner?

3.   _____ house is this?

4.   _____ are you doing this evening?

5.   _____ did you meet yesterday?

ISBN: 978-1-897457-04-7

Root Words and Building New Words

F. Fill in the chart below to create new words from the words given. A prefix is given for the first new word and a suffix for the second.

Words can be altered by adding a prefix or a suffix or by changing the form of the word.

Word	With Prefixes	With Suffixes
1. change	ex ➡	able ➡
2. print	im ➡	ing ➡
3. polite	im ➡	ness ➡
4. believe	dis ➡	able ➡
5. patient	im ➡	ce ➡
6. real	un ➡	istic ➡
7. definite	in ➡	ly ➡
8. behave	mis ➡	iour ➡
9. appoint	dis ➡	ment ➡
10. sincere	in ➡	ity ➡

G. The root words below have been changed to make new words in the passage. Write the new word from the passage beside its root word.

1. transform _____

2. warn _____

3. create _____

4. wide _____

5. diverse _____

6. tropics _____

7. beauty _____

8. depend _____

ISBN: 978-1-897457-04-7

Unit 5

The Atlas

An atlas is a scale model of the Earth. It helps us look at the entire Earth. There are seven large land masses called continents. These include: Africa, Asia, South America, North America, Europe, Antarctica, and Australia. The water surface of the Earth is divided into five oceans: Atlantic, Pacific, Indian, Arctic, and Antarctic.

The imaginary line that circles the globe halfway between the North Pole and the South Pole is called the equator. A similar imaginary circle that runs north-south and passes through Greenwich is called the prime meridian. Lines of latitude (called parallels because they run parallel to the equator) run east-west and measure distances north and south of the equator. Lines of longitude (called meridians) run north-south and measure distances east and west of the prime meridian.

Distances on an atlas are measured in degrees (°). Degrees are further divided into minutes. There are 60 minutes for each degree. The equator is at 0° while the North Pole is at 90°. Therefore, the distance from the North Pole to the South Pole is 180° in total. Similarly, the prime meridian is at 0° and distances east and west are between 0° and 180° in both directions for a total of 360° (180° E and 180° W). Therefore, it is easy to plot an exact location on a map. Toronto, for example, is at roughly 80° west of the prime meridian and 45° north of the equator.

ISBN 978-1-897457-04-7

Recalling Details

A.   Match the facts in Column A with the meanings in Column B.

Column A

Column B

1.   continents   _____

2.   degrees   _____

3.   60   _____

4.   7 of these   _____

5.   longitude and
     latitude   _____

6.   equator   _____

7.   meridians   _____

8.   5 of these   _____

9.   parallels   _____

10.   prime meridian   _____

A.   oceans

B.   located at 0° longitude

C.   run parallel to the equator

D.   minutes for each degree

E.   measurement of longitude and
     latitude

F.   continents

G.   land masses

H.   east-west/north-south lines

I.   lines of longitude

J.   located at 0° latitude

Content Quiz

B.   Can you list the oceans of the world?

1.   _____   2.   _____   3.   _____

4.   _____   5.   _____

**C.   Underline the seven continents. Be careful – some of these are
      countries, not continents.**

New Zealand   Australasia   Venezuela   Australia   United States

Central America   China   Asia   Europe   Holland   Canada   Africa

South America   North America   Mexico   Antarctica

ISBN: 978-1-897457-04-7

The Direct Object

- A **Direct Object** in a sentence is the noun that receives the action of the verb.
  Example: John kicked the soccer ball into the net.
  In this case, the object would be the "ball" since it is the noun receiving the action of the verb "kicked".

D.   Underline the direct objects in the sentences below.

1. Bill took his brother to the baseball game.

2. Paul lifted the cabinet by himself.

3. The girls played tennis in the morning.

4. Don't wake me up.

5. The teacher collected the test papers.

6. The police officer arrested the thief.

7. The plane carried the passengers across the ocean.

8. In the morning, they ate breakfast together.

9. She ironed her dress and polished her shoes.

10. The sun warmed the flowers.

E.   Complete each sentence by placing a direct object following the verb.

1. The students in the school enjoyed _____ .

2. To make the room tidy, they cleaned _____ .

3. Her mother baked _____ .

4. The boys in the band played _____ .

5. The talented carpenter built _____ .

ISBN: 978-1-897457-04-7

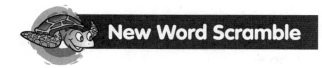

New Word Scramble

F. **The following scrambled words are from the reading passage. Use the definition clue to unscramble each of the words.**

1. **retine**	☐ n ☐ i ☐ ☐	the whole thing
2. **oelgb**	☐ l ☐ ☐ e	the Earth
3. **riccles**	☐ ☐ ☐ c ☐ e ☐	goes round
4. **ceaxt**	☐ x ☐ ☐ t	precise, accurate
5. **lasec**	☐ ☐ a ☐ e	the same but much smaller
6. **mirep**	p ☐ ☐ ☐ e	first, most important

CHALLENGE

G. **Choose four of the new words in (F) and use each one in a sentence.**

1. _____

_____

2. _____

_____

3. _____

_____

4. _____

_____

ISBN: 978-1-897457-04-7

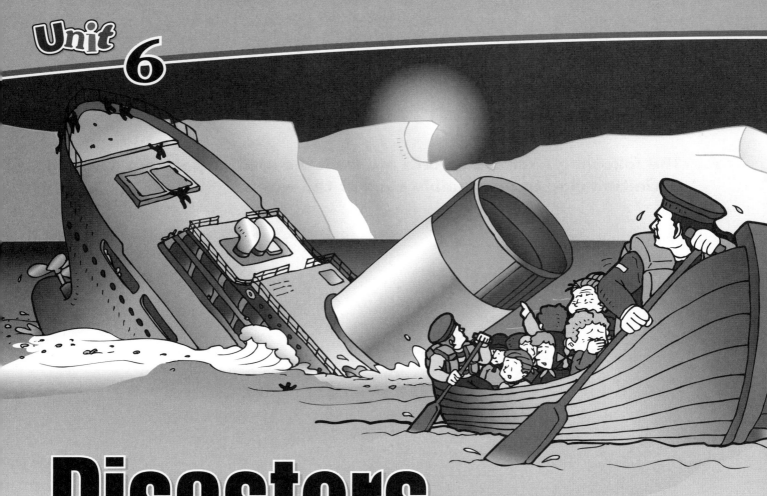

Disasters
at Sea (1)

While the sinking of the Titanic is the most notorious shipwreck of all time, there are numerous other marine tragedies. The sinking of the Lusitania, the Empress of Ireland, and the Britannic are other notable disasters at sea.

On April 10, 1912, the Titanic departed on her maiden voyage from Southampton, England heading across the Atlantic to New York City. The Titanic was the most luxurious passenger liner of its time. The 2,227 passengers were to enjoy the many luxuries of the Titanic, which included a gymnasium, a heated swimming pool, elegant dining rooms, stately passenger rooms, and a grand ballroom.

Four days after leaving Southampton, a lookout by the name of Frederick Fleet spotted an iceberg approaching out of the fog. A minute later, the iceberg struck the hull of the Titanic causing severe damage. In less than three hours, the ship split in two and the bow plunged into the sea.

The ship was not equipped with enough lifeboats to carry all the passengers. When the ship was going down, many passengers were left helplessly floating in the dark, cold waters of the Atlantic. Over 1,500 died that fateful night.

ISBN: 978-1-897457-04-7

The Main Idea

• The **Main Idea** of a paragraph is the basic topic being discussed.

A. Check the statement that gives the main idea of each paragraph.

1. **Paragraph One**

   A. _____ The sinking of the Titanic is the most notorious shipwreck of all time.
   B. _____ There are other notable marine disasters besides the Titanic.
   C. _____ The Lusitania is a famous ship.

2. **Paragraph Two**

   A. _____ The Titanic was on her maiden voyage.
   B. _____ The Titanic was a luxurious passenger liner.
   C. _____ The Titanic had a heated swimming pool.

3. **Paragraph Three**

   A. _____ Frederick Fleet was a lookout on the Titanic.
   B. _____ An iceberg struck the Titanic.
   C. _____ The bow of the Titanic plunged into the sea.

4. **Paragraph Four**

   A. _____ The ship did not have enough lifeboats.
   B. _____ Passengers were floating in the Atlantic.
   C. _____ Over 1,500 passengers died.

Using Facts: Your Opinion

B. Answer the following question with your opinion based on the facts of the story.

How was the Titanic poorly prepared for emergency? What extra precautions should have been taken?

_____

_____

_____

ISBN: 978-1-897457-04-7

Unit 6

The Indirect Object

- An **Indirect Object** is to whom or what the action of the verb is directed.
  Example: He gave me the money.
  The direct object is "money" and the indirect object is "me".

C. **The underlined words are the direct objects of the sentences. Circle the indirect objects.**

1. Joe is throwing his dog <u>a bone</u>.

2. She gave me <u>the instructions</u>.

3. Linda passed Cathy <u>the ball</u>.

4. The man paid the mechanic <u>$100</u>.

5. We sent him <u>the money</u> in an envelope.

6. Paul sent his mother <u>flowers</u> on Mother's Day.

7. Give him <u>a call</u> if you want to get a ride to school.

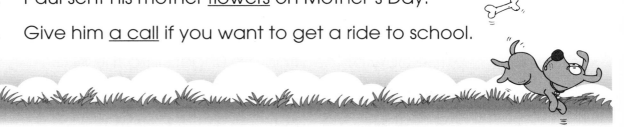

The Direct Object and the Indirect Object

D. **For each case, use the given words to compose a sentence that has a direct object and an indirect object.**

1. offered   him   ride

_____

2. letter   sent   her

_____

3. father   asked   reason

_____

ISBN: 978-1-897457-04-7

Synonyms

- A **Synonym** is a word that has the same meaning as another word and could be used in place of that word.

E.   For each of the eight words from the passage, circle the best synonym.

1.	numerous		few many numbered most
2.	tragedies		incidents occurrences disasters events
3.	departed		arrived left dropped flew
4.	luxurious		expensive cheap nice important
5.	elegant		fancy neat tidy shiny
6.	grand		small loud large necessary
7.	spotted		dotted looked saw watched
8.	plunged		fell floated drifted punched

F.   Pretend that you are a reporter giving an account of the sinking of the Titanic. Write your radio broadcast below.

Use as many of the new words above as you can. The first sentence is the beginning of your announcement.

This is _____ of WEBK Radio. I am reporting live from the scene of the sinking of the Titanic.

_____

_____

_____

_____

_____

ISBN: 978-1-897457-04-7

BRITANNIC

Just two years after the Titanic tragedy, the Empress of Ireland, another upscale passenger ship, sank in the St. Lawrence River just east of Québec City. In the early morning of May 30, 1914, a Norwegian coal ship, the Storstad, rammed the Empress of Ireland in thick fog. It took only 14 minutes for the liner to sink. Of the 1,477 passengers on board, 1,012 died.

Three years after the Titanic tragedy, another luxury liner, the Lusitania, met the same fate. The Lusitania transported passengers from North America to Ireland. Although it was a British ship, many of the passengers were Americans. In 1914, a war broke out between the British and the Germans. On May 7, 1915, a German submarine torpedoed the Lusitania off the southern coast of Ireland. The ship sank completely in 18 minutes. Of the 1,959 people on board, 1,195 lost their lives.

On November 21, 1916, the Britannic sank while cruising in the Mediterranean Sea. The Britannic was a hospital ship serving the soldiers of World War I. According to the rules of war, it was to be safe from attack. It was believed that the ship either hit a German mine or was struck by a torpedo. It took 55 minutes for the Britannic to sink, giving time for many passengers to abandon the ship. Of the over 1,000 people on board, only 30 died.

The Titanic, the Empress of Ireland, the Lusitania, and the Britannic were all closely related in structure. Sadly, they all suffered the same fate.

Disasters at Sea (2)

ISBN: 978-1-897457-04-7

Recalling Facts

A. Place "T" for true statements or "F" for false ones.

1. The Lusitania was luckier than the Titanic. _____

2. The Lusitania travelled from North America to Ireland. _____

3. Most of the passengers on the Lusitania were British. _____

4. An American submarine crashed into the Lusitania. _____

5. The Empress of Ireland sank in 1914. _____

6. The Empress of Ireland was a Norwegian coal ship. _____

7. It was foggy when the Empress of Ireland was hit. _____

8. The Britannic sank in the Atlantic Ocean. _____

9. The Britannic was a hospital ship. _____

10. The majority of the passengers on the Britannic died. _____

Comparing Facts

B. Complete the chart to compare the three ships.

		Empress of Ireland	Lusitania	Britannic
1.	Date of sinking			
2.	Type of ship			
3.	Where it sank			
4.	Why it sank			
5.	Time taken to sink			
6.	Lives lost			

ISBN: 978-1-897457-04-7

The Basic Sentence

- A **Basic Sentence** is made up of two parts: the Subject and the Predicate.
- The subject contains a noun that performs the action in the sentence or is the thing being described by the predicate.

Example: The children laughed out loud at the joke.

The subject is "the children"; the predicate is "laughed out loud at the joke".

C. Draw a vertical line separating the subject and the predicate in each sentence below.

1. He played with his dog in the backyard.

2. His parents told him to be home by 4:30.

3. His birthday presents were hidden under the bed.

4. Melanie's best friend is Sandra.

5. Two and two make four.

6. They played hide-and-seek in the old house.

D. Match the subjects with the appropriate predicates.

Subject

1. The ballerina
2. Both his parents
3. The school team
4. Professional athletes
5. The pilot

Predicate

A. won all their games.

B. often get injured.

C. sat in the cockpit.

D. had to be on her toes.

E. went to work each day.

ISBN: 978-1-897457-04-7

 **Synonyms**

E.   Substitute each underlined word with an appropriate synonym.

> delicious   elegant   swiftly   depressing
> drenched   spacious   frequently   chilly
> elated   scrumptious

1.   Her dress was <u>nice</u>.   _____

2.   The rooms in the house were <u>big</u>.   _____

3.   The food was <u>good</u>.   _____

4.   She talked <u>often</u>.   _____

5.   Her clothes were <u>wet</u>.   _____

6.   The dessert was <u>tasty</u>.   _____

7.   The children were <u>happy</u>.   _____

8.   It was a <u>cold</u> night.   _____

9.   It was a <u>sad</u> movie.   _____

10.   He ran <u>fast</u>.   _____

F.   Choose four of the words in the list in (E) and write a sentence for each.

1.   _____

2.   _____

3.   _____

4.   _____

ISBN: 978-1-897457-04-7

Unit 8

Ancient civilizations discovered by experimenting that certain plants contained remedies to illness. They also discovered that some plants contained poisons that were often fatal. Once discovered, plants that were medicinal were cultivated in special gardens. This was the origin of herbal medicine as we know it today.

Plants – *Nature's Medicine*

There are a number of plants that produce medicines. One of the most popular natural medicines in wide use today is ginseng, an ancient Chinese herbal remedy that dates back 5,000 years.

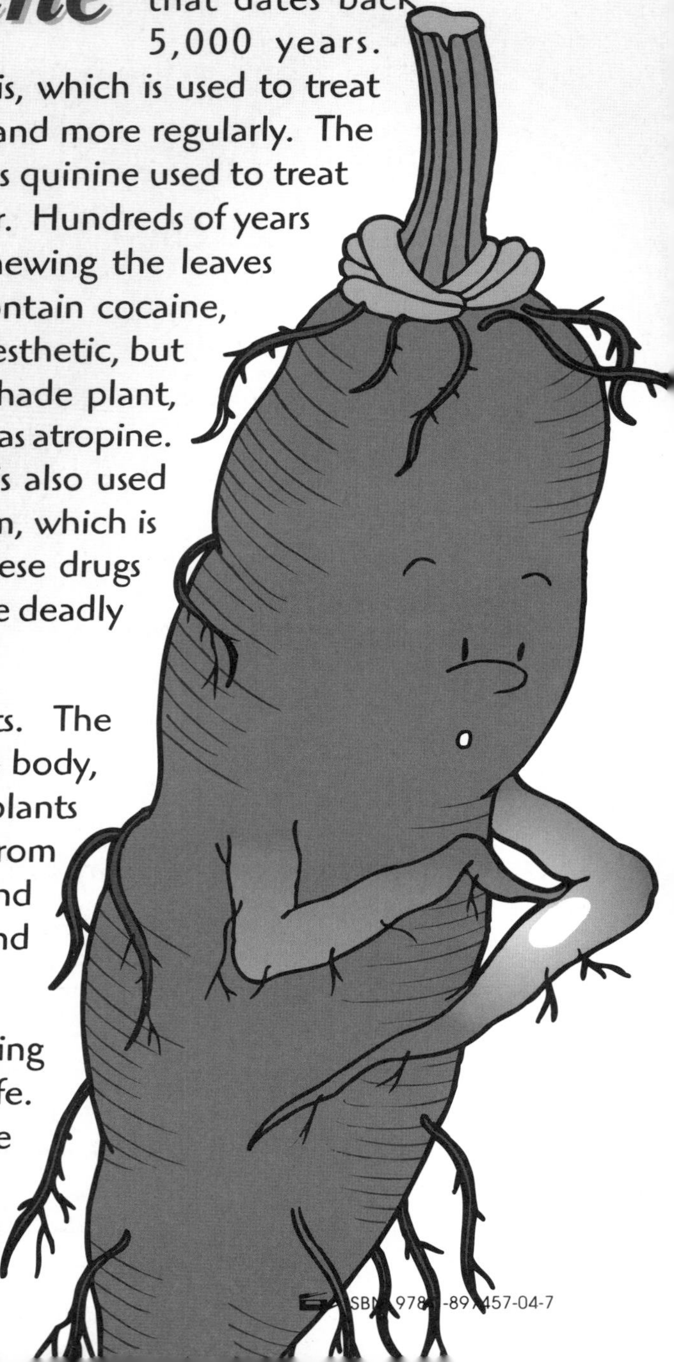

The leaves of the foxglove plant produce digitalis, which is used to treat heart conditions. It helps the heart beat slower and more regularly. The bark of the South American cinchona tree gives us quinine used to treat malaria. Quinine is also used to make tonic water. Hundreds of years ago, South American Indians discovered that chewing the leaves of the coca plant relieved pain. These leaves contain cocaine, which, in controlled doses, can be a valuable anaesthetic, but in large doses can be deadly. The deadly nightshade plant, also known as Belladonna, produces a drug known as atropine. This drug is used to treat stomach ailments and is also used in eye surgery. The opium poppy produces opium, which is turned into morphine, codeine, and heroin. These drugs act as pain killers when given by doctors but can be deadly if taken without control.

Some plants are used for topical treatments. The term "topical" refers to use on the outside of the body, typically on the skin. Two of the most popular plants are aloe vera and jojoba. The creams produced from these plants are sold at cosmetic counters around the world. They are believed to reduce dryness and skin damage from sunburn.

Like our ancient ancestors, we are discovering the benefits of natural medicines in our everyday life. Creams, herbal teas, and food additives are some of the common uses of plant medicines today.

ISBN 978-1-897457-04-7

Recalling Facts

A. Match the facts from the reading passage with the words.

1. herbal medicine   _____
2. ginseng   _____
3. foxglove plant   _____
4. coca leaves   _____
5. Belladonna   _____
6. opium poppy   _____
7. topical   _____
8. aloe vera/jojoba   _____

A. skin creams are made from these

B. chew these to relieve pain

C. also known as deadly nightshade

D. produces powerful drugs for killing pain

E. Chinese herbal remedy

F. digitalis (heart drug) is made from this

G. general term for plants used as medicine

H. refers to outside the body

Reviewing Exact Details

B. Place "T" for true or "F" for false beside each statement.

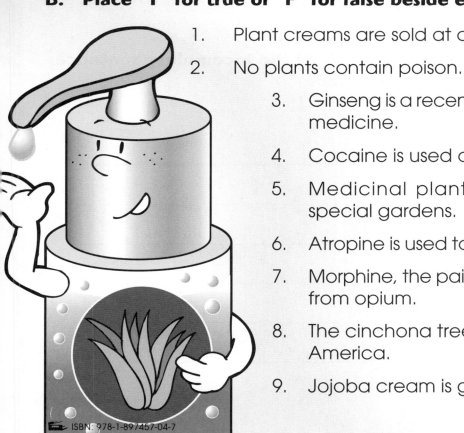

1. Plant creams are sold at cosmetic counters.   _____

2. No plants contain poison.   _____

3. Ginseng is a recent discovery in plant medicine.   _____

4. Cocaine is used as an anaesthetic.   _____

5. Medicinal plants were grown in special gardens.   _____

6. Atropine is used to treat headaches.   _____

7. Morphine, the pain killer, is produced from opium.   _____

8. The cinchona tree is native to North America.   _____

9. Jojoba cream is good for the skin.   _____

ISBN: 978-1-897457-04-7

 Building Simple Sentences

C. **Provide a suitable subject for each sentence. Try to include descriptive words to suit the predicate meaning.**

Example: The excited boy jumped up and down. The word "excited" helps explain why the boy (subject) jumped up and down.

1. _____ built the swing all on his own.

2. _____ was covered in paint.

3. _____ went to the shopping mall.

4. _____ were worried about the Math test.

5. _____ flew over the fence and broke a window.

6. _____ always shares his candy.

7. _____ came first in the race.

8. _____ arrived in Canada for the first time.

D. **Compose a predicate ending for each of the incomplete sentences below. Try to include descriptive details.**

1. The fearless firefighter _____ .

2. The playful kitten _____ .

3. The entire school _____ .

4. The sad little boy _____ .

5. The entire audience _____ .

6. Most of the players on the team _____ .

ISBN: 978-1-897457-04-7

Antonyms

- **Antonyms**, unlike synonyms, are opposite in meaning.

E. Solve the antonym puzzle with the underlined words in the passage.

Across

A. rare
B. unknown
C. new
D. lively
E. faster
F. health

Down

1. hurts
2. worthless
3. destroys
4. unsure
5. poisonous
6. damages

Remember, you are looking for the underlined words that are opposites of the clue words.

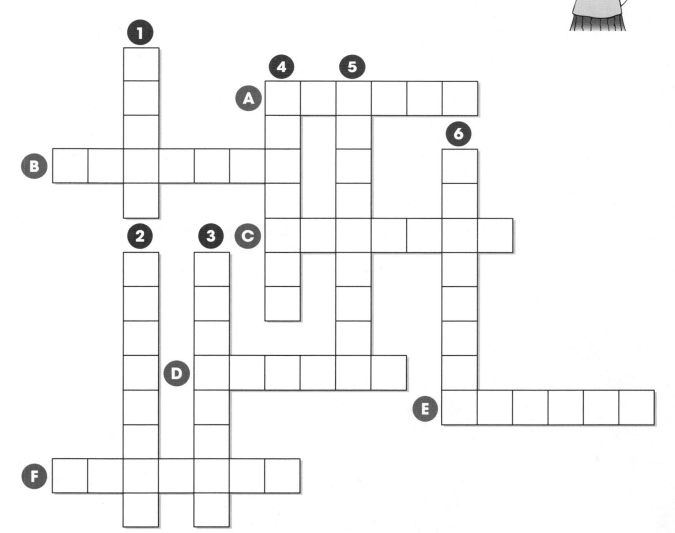

ISBN: 978-1-897457-04-7

Education in the Renaissance

In the Renaissance Period (1500-1650), people became interested in higher education. They wanted to learn the ancient languages such as Greek and Latin and study mathematics, science, and philosophy. Many universities were founded during the 16th century.

University education was a privilege of the rich. Girls were not allowed to attend and poor people could not afford to go. A member of a wealthy family could attend university at the age of ten. He might study at various universities and since the teaching was all done in Latin, it didn't matter in which country he studied. It was not unusual for a young boy to study one year in Italy and another in France without speaking either French or Italian.

It was possible in the 16th century to complete university without learning how to read or write. Since books were handwritten, there was not enough to give one to each student. Often, only the teacher had a book. He would read to the students who would memorize what he said. Tests were oral, not written. In fact, many students finished school without ever writing a word!

For the not so wealthy, grammar schools were established in towns. They learned basic grammar and mathematics, and took part in Bible study. At home, girls learned sewing, cooking, dancing, and the basics of taking care of a household. Poor children never attended school.

The Renaissance was a time when scholars did not simply accept what they were told. They conducted scientific experiments in search of answers to the mysteries of the universe. Copernicus calculated that the Earth revolved around the sun but was afraid to publish his works for fear that the Church would punish him. Galileo later supported this theory. The watch, the telescope, and the submarine were some inventions of this period.

ISBN: 978-1-897457-04-7

Making Inferences

- An **Inference** is an idea you get from the information provided in the reading passage that you believe could be factual or true.

A. For each question below, give your answer based on the information you have read in the passage.

1. If it was possible to graduate from university during the Renaissance without having learned how to read or write, how and what did students learn?

   _____

   _____

   _____

2. Why were girls not allowed to go to university during the Renaissance Period?

   _____

   _____

   _____

3. Why could the Renaissance be called "a period of curiosity"?

   _____

   _____

   _____

4. Why was Copernicus afraid that the Church would punish him for publishing his ideas about the universe?

   _____

   _____

   _____

ISBN: 978-1-897457-04-7

Constructing Simple Sentences

Try and find the verb first. Then build the sentence.

B. Put the words in order to construct a sentence.

1. candles   the   cake   had   nine   it   on   birthday

_____

2. the   around   mouse   the   chased   cat   room   the

_____

3. son   fishing   his   went   and   the   lake   in   father   the

_____

4. ended   school   began   when   holidays   summer   the

_____

Using Adjectives and Adverbs

C. Fill in the blanks with adjectives and adverbs to make the passage more interesting.

Since it was a _1._____ summer day, James and Philip ran

_2._____ to the _3._____ swimming pool and jumped into

the water. The _4._____ lifeguard told them not to play

_5._____ in case there was an accident. Once they had cooled

off, they went to buy a _6._____ ice cream cone. They ate their

cones _7._____ and decided that they would swim _8._____

during the summer.

ISBN: 978-1-897457-04-7

Similes

- A **Simile** is a descriptive comparison between two objects that have similar qualities. These two objects are linked by the word "like" or "as". Often, animals and nature are used to form similes.

  Example: He ran like the wind.

  Here the movement of running is compared to the movement of the wind.

D. Complete the following simile comparisons.

1. He was as tall as _____ .

2. She jumped like _____ .

3. The plane flew like _____ .

4. The moon shone like _____ .

5. The actress danced like _____ .

6. The house was as large as _____ .

7. The baby was as playful as _____ .

8. The melon was as sweet as _____ .

E. Create the first part of the simile for each description below.

1. She was as _____ as a lamb.

2. He was as _____ as an ox.

3. She was as _____ as a cat.

4. He was as _____ as a pig.

5. She _____ like a tortoise.

6. He _____ like a frog.

7. She _____ like a fish.

8. He _____ like a deer.

ISBN: 978-1-897457-04-7

Recalling Details

A. Place "T" for true or "F" for false on the line beside each statement.

1. Some animals can survive in harsh environments. _____

2. Adaptations can be regional or behavioural. _____

3. Arctic hares have white coats all year round. _____

4. Some raccoons live in attics and basements. _____

5. Human beings can control whether or not their heart beats. _____

6. The heart has five chambers. _____

7. A child's heart would beat 80 to 100 times per minute. _____

8. Christian Barnard was the first heart transplant recipient. _____

9. The first heart transplant recipient died 19 days after the operation. _____

10. Some butterflies use their colour as a camouflage. _____

11. Most butterflies feed on nectar. _____

12. There are three stages of the butterfly's life cycle. _____

13. The Earth's surface is made up of 7 large land masses. _____

14. The water surface of the Earth is divided into 6 oceans. _____

15. Grid lines on a map that run east-west are called lines of longitude. _____

16. Lines of longitude are called meridians. _____

17. The equator divides the Earth in halves. _____

ISBN: 978-1-897457-04-7

B.   Circle the letters of the correct answers.

1.   The Titanic was thought to be

A. the fastest ship.   B. the largest ship.   C. unsinkable.

2.   The Titanic left Southampton to go to

A. Boston.   B. New York City.   C. Montreal.

3.   The number of people that died on the Titanic was

A. over 1,500.   B. fewer than 1,000.   C. over 2,200.

4.   The Lusitania transported passengers between

A. England and   B. England and   C. Ireland and
   France.   Germany.   America.

5.   The Lusitania sank because

A. it hit an iceberg.   B. it was torpedoed.   C. it had a faulty
                                                             engine.

6.   The Britannic was a

A. hospital ship.   B. cargo ship.   C. battleship.

7.   A popular herbal medicine used today is

A. tree bark.   B. rice.   C. ginseng.

8.   Topical treatment refers to plants that help heal the

A. outer body.   B. inner soul.   C. vital organs.

9.   In the Renaissance Period, women were not allowed to

A. get married.   B. have children.   C. go to university.

10.   In the 16th century, one could finish university without

A. being able to write.   B. going to school.   C. speaking French.

11.   In the Renaissance Period, scholars were interested in

A. plant life.   B. science.   C. leisure.

ISBN: 978-1-897457-04-7

Nouns and Verbs

There may be more than one verb or noun in a sentence. Also, the noun does not have to be the subject.

C. Underline the nouns and put parentheses ( ) around the verbs in the following sentences.

1. She likes eating ice cream on a hot day.

2. He tripped over his shoelace and fell down the stairs.

3. The boys and girls played in the same yard.

4. Jim, John, and Sam walked to school together.

5. Linda is five years older than Susan.

6. The neighbours held a garage sale on their street.

7. Winter is a long and cold season.

8. Time is wasted when we do nothing.

9. The clock struck three and the school bell rang.

Adjectives and Adverbs

Adjectives describe nouns while adverbs describe verbs.

D. Underline the adjectives and circle the adverbs in the sentences below.

1. The blazing sun sank slowly in the west.

2. The happy child opened her birthday present quickly.

3. Slowly but surely, the skilled skiers slipped down the hill.

4. Karen, a tall girl, was chosen immediately for the basketball team.

5. He ran swiftly between the stone obstacles on the sandy beach.

ISBN: 978-1-897457-04-7

Pronouns

A pronoun is used in place of a noun or to refer to a noun used previously in a sentence.

E. Fill in the blanks in the following sentences with pronouns.

1. Lisa's parents watched him/her _____ playing.

2. He/She _____ likes to eat her lunch outdoors.

3. John told we/me _____ about his problem.

4. They/We _____ bought themselves ice cream cones.

5. Susan asked when she/her _____ would be allowed to go home.

Direct and Indirect Objects

F. Underline the direct object and circle the indirect object in each sentence.

A direct object receives the action of the verb; an indirect object is to whom or what the action is directed.

1. He gave me the ball.

2. We sent Grandma a postcard.

3. The parents gave their son a new bicycle.

4. The quarterback threw the running back the ball for a touchdown.

5. The teacher gave us one more chance to finish our work.

The Subject and Predicate

The subject is the performer of the action or is the thing described by the predicate.

G. Match each subject with a suitable predicate.

1. The Toronto Maple Leafs _____   A. could not stop in time.

2. The driver _____   B. can be dangerous if you fall.

3. Skiing _____   C. both made the swim team.

4. Bob and Billy _____   D. practised in the old arena.

5. People in Nunavut _____   E. prepare for a long and cold winter.

ISBN: 978-1-897457-04-7

New Words from the Reading Passages

H. Match the words from the passages with the definitions.

1. origin   _____   A.   unaware, no knowledge of

2. transparent   _____   B.   the beginning of, starting point

3. eerie   _____   C.   all the time, regularly

4. oblivious   _____   D.   disorder, confusion

5. chaos   _____   E.   expensive, tasteful, luxurious

6. consistently   _____   F.   well-known, well-liked

7. resume   _____   G.   continue, carry on

8. elegant   _____   H.   left, went away

9. departed   _____   I.   see-through

10. popular   _____   J.   scary, weird, haunted

Words Often Confused

I. Choose the correct word for the meaning of each sentence.

1. She wrote in her dairy/diary _____ daily.

2. He came forth/fourth _____ in the race.

3. She accomplished an amazing feet/feat _____ .

4. He couldn't decide weather/whether _____ or not to play.

5. The enemies fought a duel/dual _____ .

6. He was sitting so far away he couldn't here/hear _____ .

ISBN: 978-1-897457-04-7

Forming New Words

J.   Add a prefix or suffix to each of the words to make a new word.

1. arrange _____
2. organize _____
3. view _____
4. connect _____
5. mind _____
6. appoint _____
7. satisfied _____
8. create _____
9. belief _____
10. care _____
11. rely _____
12. depend _____
13. distant _____
14. happy _____
15. prior _____
16. known _____

Descriptive Language

K.   Change the words in parentheses to the more descriptive words from below.

| drenched | hilarious | bitterly | antique |
| kind | spacious | delicious | pelting |

1. Dinner was (good) _____ .
2. The movie was (very funny) _____ .
3. The winter night was (very) _____ cold.
4. The (nice) _____ person helped the lady.
5. They were (wet) _____ from the (amount of) _____ rain.
6. The (big) _____ room was filled with (old) _____ furniture.

ISBN: 978-1-897457-04-7

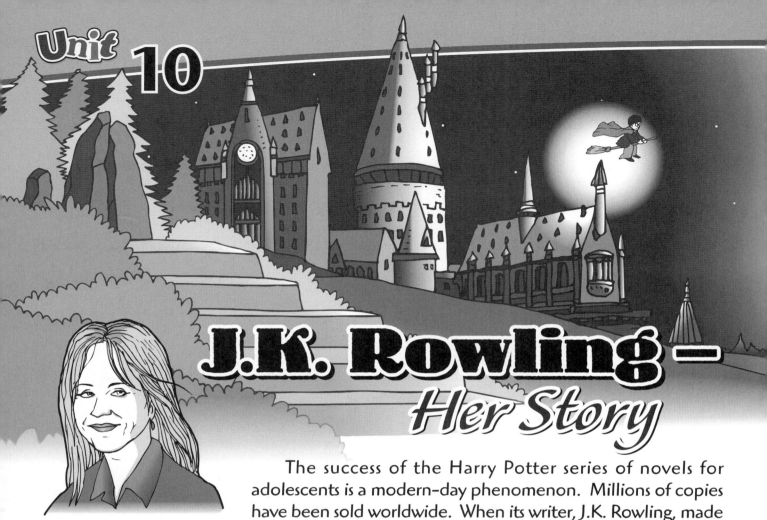

J.K. Rowling – Her Story

The success of the Harry Potter series of novels for adolescents is a modern-day phenomenon. Millions of copies have been sold worldwide. When its writer, J.K. Rowling, made a personal appearance in Toronto at the SkyDome, she drew the largest crowd ever recorded for a public reading session.

J.K. Rowling is now enjoying fame and wealth but it wasn't always that way. When she began to write the first Harry Potter book, she was a single mother of an infant daughter living on social assistance. She lived in a tiny rented apartment in Edinburgh, Scotland. She spent time in a local café where she wrote her first story, *Harry Potter and the Philosopher's Stone*. This novel completely changed her life.

As a child, J.K. Rowling loved English literature. She wrote her first real story at the age of 6. It was then that she decided that she wanted to become a writer. She thought writing would be the best occupation because she would be getting paid to do something she enjoyed.

J.K. Rowling isn't absolutely sure where she gets the ideas for the Harry Potter stories. The odd names for her characters come from a variety of sources. Some of her characters are loosely based on real people that she knows. However, once she starts to develop the characters, they become different from their source. The Potter stories are not based on Rowling's life, although most authors put a little of themselves into their writing.

Through the Harry Potter series, J.K. Rowling has been credited with increasing the interest in reading for children around the world.

ISBN: 978-1-897457-04-7

The Main Idea

A. **Circle the letter of the most appropriate statement that gives the main idea of each paragraph.**

Paragraph One

A. J.K. Rowling enjoys writing.

B. J.K. Rowling is a popular author.

C. Harry Potter novels are interesting.

D. Harry Potter is an interesting character.

Paragraph Two

A. J.K. Rowling is wealthy.

B. J.K. Rowling was a poor author.

C. J.K. Rowling drinks coffee.

D. Harry Potter saved her life.

Paragraph Three

A. Six-year-olds can be writers.

B. Write when you're young.

C. J.K. Rowling loved literature.

D. Don't write unless you get paid.

Paragraph Four

A. J.K. Rowling writes about people that she knows.

B. The characters in her books are sometimes based on real people.

C. Her novels are based strictly on her life.

D. Her characters are all made up.

Your Opinion

B. **Answer the question.**

Why is J.K. Rowling credited with changing the reading habits of children around the world?

_____

_____

_____

ISBN: 978-1-897457-04-7

Prepositions

- A **Preposition** helps connect a noun or pronoun to another part of the sentence. It also connects a verb to other words in the sentence.

  Example: The students in the class read quietly.

  The word "in" connects the subject, students, to the class. Now we know that they are the students from the class.

  Example: He placed his hat on the hook.

  The word "on" connects the verb "placed" to the word "hook", which is where the hat is placed.

C. **Choose eight prepositions and use each to create a sentence. After each sentence, place "N" if the preposition connects a noun to other words and "V" if it connects a verb to other words.**

after	down	into	under	inside	near	without
until	beside	at	above	around	below	of
on	for	from	before	among	about	with

1. The children played baseball in the yard.   (V)

2. _____ (   )

3. _____ (   )

4. _____ (   )

5. _____ (   )

6. _____ (   )

7. _____ (   )

8. _____ (   )

9. _____ (   )

ISBN: 978-1-897457-04-7

Making Opposites

D. Add the proper prefixes to the words to make the opposites.

1. un/im _____ prepared
2. dis/un _____ appointed
3. dis/un _____ fair
4. un/im _____ proper
5. im/un _____ possible
6. un/dis _____ honour
7. un/dis _____ approve
8. dis/un _____ likely
9. dis/un _____ happy
10. in/un _____ complete
11. dis/un _____ necessary
12. im/un _____ perfect

Building Vocabulary

E. Change the word in parentheses in each sentence to a form that fits the sense of the sentence.

Example: John is (give) _____ away his bicycle.

You would place the word "giving" in the space, which is a form of the word "give" in parentheses.

1. Show (kind) _____ towards others.
2. It was (terrible) _____ cold outside.
3. Be (care) _____ when you go swimming.
4. They were studying the (move) _____ of the Earth.
5. The wedding was followed by a (celebrate) _____ .
6. He was very (help) _____ when he was needed.
7. It was a (beauty) _____ morning with the sunshine.
8. She could not find the (solve) _____ to the problem.

ISBN: 978-1-897457-04-7

The toys children play with today are often highly technical and electronic, and involve the use of a computer. The children of pioneer Canada, however, did not have such advanced toys and games as these. Instead, they relied on making their own toys and creating interactive games that involved simple physical action.

Although their toys were simple, pioneer children were never bored. After a hard day's work helping their parents on the homestead, they looked forward to free time for play. Many of their favourite games like blind man's bluff and hide-and-seek are still played today. A rope tied to a tree made a perfect swing and a plank over a

Games and Toys of Pioneer Canada (1)

saw-horse made an ideal seesaw. In playgrounds of today, the swing and the seesaw are still very popular. These playground favourites are perhaps better made today but are no more enjoyable than they were for pioneer children.

Nature provided not only the material for making toys but also the toy itself. A weeping willow tree beside a creek was an exciting toy. Children would swing on a willow branch over the creek and let go, creating a splash. This activity was a perfect way to cool off on a hot summer day.

Horseshoe pitching was one of the most popular games all across Canada. It was not only a game for children. Adults took this game very seriously and competitions between neighbours and towns were common.

ISBN 978-1-897457-04-7

Drawing Conclusions

- A **Conclusion** is an opinion reached after considering facts and details.

A. Draw conclusions for the following questions.

1. Why were pioneer children happy to have simple toys?

    _____

    _____

2. Why was swinging from a tree over a creek so much fun for pioneer children?

    _____

    _____

3. What facts in the story suggest that pioneer children were always busy?

    _____

    _____

4. What would lead you to believe that horseshoe pitching was a very important pastime in pioneer days?

    _____

    _____

5. How can nature and the use of one's imagination result in creating fun and interesting games?

    _____

    _____

Recalling Facts

B. Explain how you would make the following toys. Be sure to mention all the materials you would need.

1. a seesaw   _____

2 . a swing   _____

ISBN: 978-1-897457-04-7

Prepositions and Objects

- A **Preposition** is often followed by a noun acting as object of the preposition.
  Example: He climbed over the fence.
  The preposition is "over" and "fence" is the noun, object of the preposition.

C. Underline the object of the preposition in each sentence.

1. The clouds flew across the sky.

2. In the morning, she went jogging.

3. They ate lunch beside the pond.

4. Within the school, there are many different students.

5. After the rain, the road was slippery.

D. Finish each rhyme by adding the appropriate object of the preposition.

1. The cow jumped over the _____ .

2. Little Miss Muffet sat on her _____ .

3. Jack and Jill went up the _____ .

4. Humpty Dumpty sat on a _____ .

5. Hickory Dickory Dock, the mouse ran up the _____ .

E. Create sentences, using these prepositions and objects.

1. _____ around the block.

2. _____ beneath the ground.

3. After the game, _____ .

4. _____ into the closet.

5. Before lunch, _____ .

6. _____ between the houses.

(54)

ISBN: 978-1-897457-04-7

Poet's Corner

- When the 1st and 2nd lines of a poem rhyme, and the 3rd and 4th lines rhyme, the poem is following an "aa/bb" rhyming scheme. Lines of poetry placed together form a verse.

Example: The morning sun shines <u>bright</u>
Day replaces <u>night</u>
Flowers awake from their <u>sleep</u>
Birds sing cheep, <u>cheep</u>.

F. Use the "aa/bb" rhyming scheme to compose a two-verse poem or two one-verse poems.

Do you want to become a poet? Here are some rhyming words to work with.

high/try/sigh/fly/sky/sly　　long/song/strong　　ate/plate
mouse/house　　feed/need/seed

Title: _____

_____

_____

_____

_____

free/tree/see/sea/me
same/name/tame/came/fame

Title: _____

_____

_____

_____

_____

ISBN: 978-1-897457-04-7

Games and Toys of Pioneer Canada (2)

Since there were no manufactured toys available to pioneer children, they had to be very creative when it came to making their own toys. A simple ball was made out of a stuffed pig's bladder, which was sturdy enough to be kicked around the field without breaking open. The name "pigskin" which referred to this type of ball is a term still in use today. Hoop rolling was also a popular game. An iron or wooden hoop and a stick were all that was needed. The challenge was to see who could keep it rolling the longest.

With Canadian winters being so cold, indoor games were important. The pioneer children did not have malls, movie theatres, or skating rinks for shelter from the winter weather. Shadow picture making was a family favourite. They would seat a family member in front of a candle and hold up a sheet of paper. A silhouette was created and then traced.

Many games were useful in helping boys and girls prepare for adult life. Girls made rag dolls and sewed clothing. These were not as perfect in form as today's Barbie but were enjoyed just as much, and valuable skills were learned. Boys went hunting and fishing with their fathers. Making a strong fishing rod out of a tree branch was an important skill. Aside from putting food on the table, fishing was a relaxing summer pastime for a pioneer boy. Boys were skilled with knives and learned the art of carving, which was useful for making toys for their younger brothers and sisters. A pocketknife could be used to make a sturdy bow and arrow set or wooden soldiers.

Pioneer life was not as fast-paced as life today. Without automobiles, travel was rare and much time was spent around the home. Therefore the pioneer children had to find things to do to occupy their time. Even though they were without television and radio, life was never dull. There was always work to do, fields and streams to play in, and the creative art of toy making to keep them busy.

ISBN: 978-1-897457-04-7

Skimming

A. Re-read the passage quickly, taking in as many facts as you can. Once you have finished that second reading, answer the questions below. Try to answer with the exact facts from the passage.

1. What was a ball made from? _____

2. What was the name of this type of ball? _____

3. What game was played with a hoop and a stick? _____

4. In the game of shadow making, what was traced? _____

5. What toy did girls make? _____

6. What was used to make a fishing rod? _____

7. Why was travel rare in pioneer days? _____

Fact or Opinion

- A **Fact** refers to information that is given exactly from the passage. An **Opinion** is your interpretation of the information in the passage.

B. For each statement below, place "F" for fact or "O" for opinion in the space provided.

1. Pioneer children were never bored. _____

2. Pioneer boys relaxed when they went fishing. _____

3. Girls could be creative when making their dolls. _____

4. A pocketknife could be used to make wooden soldiers. _____

5. There were no manufactured toys available to pioneer children. _____

ISBN: 978-1-897457-04-7

Phrases and Clauses

- A **Phrase** is a group of words forming part of a sentence. It often begins with a preposition, followed by a noun.
- A **Clause** is a group of words that includes a subject and a verb.
  Example: <u>At the age of seven</u>, Pat already played the piano well. (phrase)
  <u>When she was seven</u>, Pat already played the piano well. (clause)

C. **Check whether the underlined group of words in each sentence is a phrase or a clause.**

P   C

1. <u>In front of the stage</u> sat the judges. ____ ____

2. I was surprised <u>that she failed the test</u>. ____ ____

3. <u>During the game</u>, the fans cheered wildly. ____ ____

4. The toys <u>in the box</u> belong to Jenny, not Katie. ____ ____

5. She was moved to tears <u>when we offered to help her</u>. ____ ____

6. <u>Because he was the first to arrive</u>, he got the best seat. ____ ____

7. <u>Because of the heavy rain</u>, the baseball game was called off. ____ ____

8. <u>When we arrived at the stadium</u>, all the good seats were taken. ____ ____

D. **Complete the sentences with suitable phrases or clauses.**

1. The boy _____ hit a grand slam.

2. After _____ , they all went to Sam's place.

3. She bought this necklace because _____ .

4. The books _____ belong to our teacher.

5. During _____ , we went to buy pop and popcorn.

6. Although _____ , we chose him to be our captain.

ISBN: 978-1-897457-04-7

Anagrams

- An **Anagram** is a word in which the letters can be moved around to form another word.

  Example: The letters in "tries" can be rearranged to make "tires".

E. Make new words using the clues. Do not add letters.

rats	look up to the sky	1. _____
ocean	boat that is easy to tip	2. _____
top	cooking utensil	3. _____
cheap	soft fruit	4. _____
could	holds the rain	5. _____

Homonyms

- **Homonyms** are words that sound the same but are spelled differently and have different meanings.

F. Complete the crossword puzzles with homonyms of the words across.

1. clothing

w h e r e

2. ears

h e r e

3. tossed

t h r o u g h

4. horse's _____

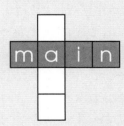

m a i n

5. no strength

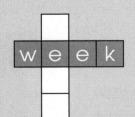

w e e k

6. wind

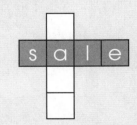

s a l e

ISBN: 978-1-897457-04-7

Medieval castles were built to house the local lords and their families. Inhabitants of the castles usually had their own apartments. Castles were equipped with a nursery, a brewhouse, a school, a chapel, a library, many bedrooms, and an elegant dining room. The dining room was furnished with a grand table for entertaining important guests. Fireplaces were numerous throughout a castle and provided the main source of heat for the apartments. Bedrooms had huge four-poster beds with soft feather pillows and thick curtains to prevent drafts.

Medieval Castles

The main purpose of a castle was protection. A lord who owned a large amount of land would lease the land out to farmers who would pay him farm produce as rent. He would offer protection against enemy attacks. In the case of an attack, villagers would gather within the castle walls and help defend the castle against invaders. As a result, villages were established near the castle.

Castles were expensive to run. It would cost millions of dollars by today's standards to build and maintain a castle. A noble in medieval times would have an income of about £1,000 or $2,500 per year. An ordinary working person might earn the equivalent of one dollar a year. But castle owners had huge expenses. They often employed 300 people to perform various tasks.

In the late 1500s, when battles became large-scale events, castles were not needed. Today, many castles in Europe have been converted into hotels and guest houses. Many castles are for sale by owners who cannot afford to occupy them. In fact, castles can be purchased for a lot less than you would expect. The real cost comes once you move in and try to pay for the household expenses.

ISBN: 978-1-897457-04-7

Finding Supporting Facts

A. For each case, place a check mark beside the information that best proves the statement given.

1. Medieval castles were not built for local people.

   A. _____ Castles were too far from the village.

   B. _____ Castles were occupied by lords and ladies.

   C. _____ Local people did not like castles.

2. Castles were well equipped.

   A. _____ There were high walls around the castle.

   B. _____ A castle had a library, a ballroom, a nursery, and a school.

   C. _____ Castles were used for defence against invaders.

3. The castle was used for protection.

   A. _____ Villagers hid inside the castle when being attacked.

   B. _____ Only the lord of the castle was protected.

   C. _____ The castle was evacuated during an attack.

4. It cost a great deal of money to run a castle.

   A. _____ Some castles employed 300 people.

   B. _____ Castles needed many repairs.

   C. _____ Castle furniture was expensive.

5. Noblemen were wealthy in medieval times.

   A. _____ Nobles worked very hard to earn money.

   B. _____ Local farmers paid heavy taxes.

   C. _____ A nobleman could have an income of £1,000 a year.

6. Fewer castles were being built.

   A. _____ There were not enough building materials.

   B. _____ There were no workers to build the castles.

   C. _____ Battles were large-scale events and fought on battlefields.

ISBN: 978-1-897457-04-7

Adjective and Adverb Phrases

- A **Phrase** is a group of words without a verb. It often begins with a preposition.
  An **Adjective Phrase** describes a noun.
  An **Adverb Phrase** describes a verb.

  Example: The gift in the box was made in Italy.
  The adjective phrase "in the box" describes the noun; the adverb phrase "in Italy" tells where the gift was made.

B. **Underline the adjective phrase in each sentence and place parentheses ( ) around the adverb phrases.**

1. In the morning, the sun rose over the cliffs.

2. The teacher of grade four sat at his desk.

3. The dog in the kennel barked loudly.

4. She hid under the desk.

5. He ran up the road and down the hill.

6. Under the rainbow, you will find a pot of gold.

Look for the prepositions first.

C. **Create sentences with adjective or adverb phrases using the given prepositions.**

1. (over) _____.

2. (beneath) _____.

3. (behind) _____.

4. (of) _____.

5. (in) _____.

6. (across) _____.

ISBN: 978-1-897457-04-7

Plural Forms

D. Circle the correct plurals and complete the rules of spelling in your own words.

1. **knife** – knifes / knives   2. **life** – lives / lifes
3. **half** – halves / halfs

Rule: For some words ending in "f" or "fe", change _____ .

4. **army** – armies / armys   5. **family** – family / families
6. **city** – citys / cities

Rule: For words ending in "y" with a consonant before the "y", drop

_____ .

7. **journey** – journies / journeys   8. **key** – keys / keies
9. **valley** – valleies / valleys

Rule: For some words ending in "y" with a vowel before the "y", add

_____ .

E. Form the plurals of the following words.

1. goose _____   2. child _____
3. foot _____   4. man _____
5. tooth _____   6. mouse _____
7. What do these words have in common in terms of their plural form?

> sheep   aircraft   deer   moose   grass   salmon

_____

ISBN: 978-1-897457-04-7

Of all the <u>organs</u> in the human body, none is more <u>vital</u> than the brain. The brain is what gives us our identity. The acts of making decisions, solving problems, and identifying objects are all the direct responsibility of the brain.

The human brain stops growing when we are about six or seven years of age. When its growth is complete, the brain weighs about 3 kilograms. The brain is the most <u>amazing</u> and <u>complex</u> object we know. It takes care of the <u>creative</u> things we do such as painting pictures, writing stories, designing buildings, or building computers. The brain processes information from all around us. When a traffic light turns red, we know not to cross the street or when a dog growls at us, we know to keep away. Much of this information is <u>stored</u> in our memory. The brain also controls all our <u>emotions</u>.

The largest part of the brain is called the cerebrum, which controls the muscles and processes sight, sound, taste, and smell messages. The left side of the cerebrum controls the right side of the body and the right side controls the left side of the body. The left side is <u>dominant</u>, which accounts for why most people are right–handed. Below the cerebrum is the cerebellum that controls balance and coordination. Near the cerebellum is the medulla oblongata that controls bodily functions such as breathing, swallowing, and vomiting. The hypothalamus controls our emotions, particularly anger and <u>fear</u>, and it controls body temperature, hunger, and thirst. The brain is also directly <u>connected</u> to our central nervous system.

The Thinking Organ

The brain has always been a <u>mystery</u> to mankind. We only know the basics of how it works. The more we study the brain and its <u>function</u>, the more we realize how complicated it is.

ISBN 978-1-897457-04-7

Recalling Details

A. Fill in the blanks in the passage below with the appropriate words.

cerebellum   nervous   left   cerebrum   organ
hypothalamus   growing   process   memory   emotions

The human brain is the most important 1._____ in the body. When we reach the age of six, the brain stops 2._____ . The main function of the brain is to 3._____ information. Much of this information is stored in our 4._____ . The brain also controls our 5._____ such as happiness and sadness. The 6._____ is the biggest part of the brain. It is above the 7._____ . Most people are right-handed because the 8._____ side of the brain is dominant. The 9._____ controls emotions and body temperature. The brain is connected to our central 10._____ system.

B. Match the facts from the passage with the descriptions or definitions.

1. 3 kilograms   _____   A. controls hunger and thirst
2. cerebrum   _____   B. controls right side of body
3. left side of brain   _____   C. controls balance and coordination
4. cerebellum   _____   D. largest part of the brain
5. medulla oblongata _____   E. weight of the brain
6. hypothalamus   _____   F. controls bodily functions

Your Opinion

C. Why do you think that the brain is still a mystery to scientists today?

_____

_____

ISBN: 978-1-897457-04-7

Conjunctions

- **Conjunctions** are words that join words, phrases, and clauses in a sentence.

  Example 1: He ran _and_ jumped. (joining words)

  Example 2: I will see you after the game _or_ during lunch. (joining phrases)

  Example 3: It was a warm day _although_ the sky was cloudy. (joining clauses)

  Example 4: Paul walked home. He met a friend. → Paul walked home _and_ met a friend. (joining two sentences into one)

D.   Complete the sentences below with appropriate conjunctions.

because   while   until   so   unless
and   or   but   if   since

> Use each of the conjunctions above once only.

1.   Peter _____ Roger were on the same team.

2.   She won't wear it _____ it fits properly.

3.   He has been tired ever _____ he caught a cold.

4.   She was happy _____ it was her birthday.

5.   Either Sheila _____ Martha will say the speech.

6.   He waited in the car _____ she went shopping.

7.   He made the decision _____ it was not popular.

8.   She will help you _____ you help yourself.

9.   They made the rules _____ it was their responsibility.

10.   She couldn't wait _____ the holidays came.

ISBN: 978-1-897457-04-7

Synonyms and Antonyms

- A **Synonym** is a word that means the same as another word.
- An **Antonym** is a word that means the opposite of another word.

E. Use the underlined words in the reading passage to complete the following word puzzles.

1. simple (antonym)

2. main (synonym)

3. boring (antonym)

4. body parts (synonym)

5. solution (antonym)

6. feelings (synonym)

7. linked (synonym)

8. courage (antonym)

9. unimportant (antonym)

10. imaginative (synonym)

11. use (synonym)

12. saved (synonym)

F. Choose two words from the puzzles above and write two sentences of your own.

Try to be creative.

1. _____

_____

2. _____

_____

ISBN: 978-1-897457-04-7

Between 1200 and 1535 CE, the Inca built the largest empire in South America, extending from the equator to the Pacific coast of Chile. The Inca were fierce warriors with a strong and powerful army. However, their prosperity came to a tragic end when the Spanish conquerors took over their territory.

The architecture of the Inca cities still amazes and puzzles most scientists. The Inca built their cities and fortresses on highlands and on the steep slopes of the Andes Mountains. Stone steps lead up to the top of the cities. The stone blocks weighing several tons are fit together so tightly that not even a razor blade can fit through them. Their homes were made from the same stone material and had grass rooftops.

The Inca developed sophisticated drainage systems and canals to expand their crop resources. They also reared llamas for meat and transportation. There were more than enough resources for everyone. The Inca had a good road system to connect the villages too. The roads were lined with barriers to prevent people from falling down the cliffs.

The Inca were not only fierce warriors but they also had a violent punishment system. People who committed theft would be severely punished. Those who committed murder would be sentenced to death.

The Inca Empire

Ironically, though, the 40,000-member army of the Inca was destroyed by a 180-member Spanish army led by Francisco Pizarro. The warriors of the Inca were simply no match for the Spanish guns. By 1535, the Inca society was completely wiped out. Now, only a few traces of Inca ways remain in the native culture as it exists today.

ISBN: 978-1-897457-04-7

Recalling Facts

A. Decide whether the following statements are true "T" or false "F".

1. The Inca Empire existed for more than 300 years. _____

2. The Inca were good warriors. _____

3. They had a legal system to uphold law and order. _____

4. The Spanish defeated the Inca warriors because they had stronger weapons. _____

5. The Inca used llamas for transportation. _____

6. The Inca architecture is like a puzzle to scientists today. _____

7. An Inca thief would be sentenced to death. _____

8. Canals were dug for irrigation. _____

9. The common people dwelled in grass huts. _____

10. The nobles lived on the highlands while the common people lived along the coast. _____

Your Opinion

B. Answer the questions.

1. Why does the architecture of Inca amaze most scientists?

   _____

   _____

2. Do you agree to the Inca punishment system? Why?

   _____

   _____

3. How could the Spanish army defeat the Inca warriors?

   _____

   _____

ISBN: 978-1-897457-04-7

Types of Sentences

- There are four main types of sentences:

  1. **Declarative** – simply makes a statement and ends with a period.
     Example: John caught the ball.

  2. **Interrogative** – asks a question and ends with a question mark.
     Example: What time is it?

  3. **Imperative** – gives a command or makes a request and ends with a period.
     Example: Answer the telephone.

  4. **Exclamatory** – expresses emotion or strong feelings and ends with an exclamation mark.
     Example: Help me, I'm falling!

C. **Punctuate each of the following sentences and state the type of sentence in the space provided.**

Don't forget to punctuate the sentences.

Decl. Declarative   **Int.** Interrogative

Imp. Imperative   **Excl.** Exclamatory

1. Look out   _____

2. Stop before it's too late   _____

3. The sun is shining today   _____

4. Whose birthday is it   _____

5. Wash your hands before dinner   _____

D. Compose your own sentences.

1. Declarative: _____

2. Interrogative: _____

3. Imperative: _____

4. Exclamatory: _____

ISBN: 978-1-897457-04-7

Crossword Puzzle

E. Complete the crossword puzzle with the words from the passage.

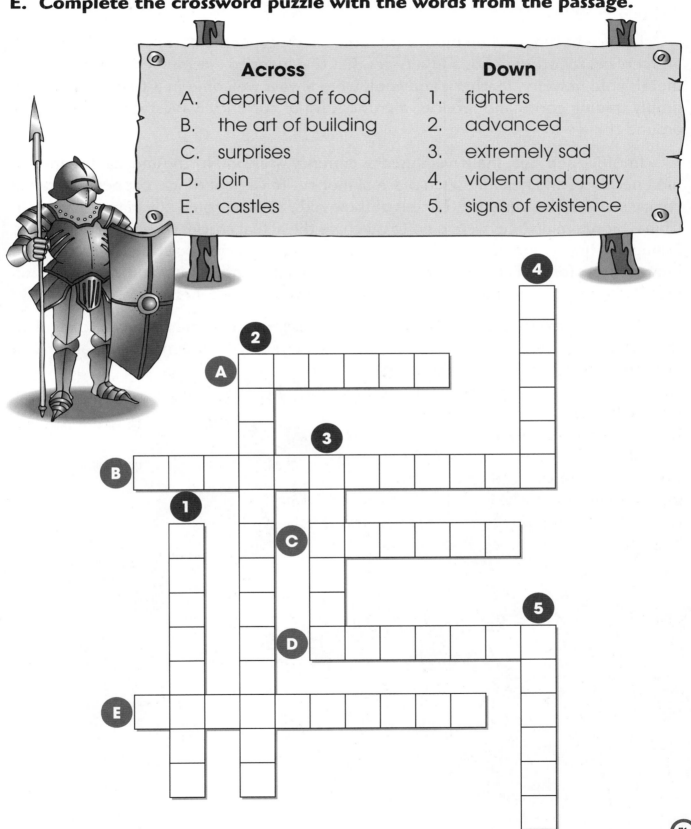

Across

A. deprived of food
B. the art of building
C. surprises
D. join
E. castles

Down

1. fighters
2. advanced
3. extremely sad
4. violent and angry
5. signs of existence

ISBN: 978-1-897457-04-7

When we want to make a purchase today, we use money. We have many options as to how we pay with money. We can use a credit card, a debit card, a personal cheque, or cash.

In ancient times, when money was non-existent, people bartered (traded) goods and services for other goods and services that they needed. Items such as shells, beads, metal, gold, jewelry, feathers, and tools were always welcome in a trade. Instead of simply trading goods and services, a crude form of currency was established by tribes around the world.

In Africa and Asia, shells were used as currency while in North America, the Indians used necklaces and headdresses in place of money. In Central Africa, copper rods called congas were used as currency. For ten of these rods, a native could buy himself a wife. In China, bronze miniatures were used to purchase the actual articles they represented. For example, a tiny replica of a tool would be used to purchase that exact tool. Probably the most popular form of currency was the use of animals. Cattle, pigs, and camels are still used today to purchase products or make payments by some tribes in Asia.

With the growth of cities, standard forms of payment became necessary to regulate the value of goods. The barter method worked nicely between individuals or in a village setting, but it lacked consistency. There was no standard by which a person could measure the value of what they were buying. It was difficult to be sure that the deal was fair. Often the one who was the shrewdest dealer profited the most. It was necessary to establish a regular system. This marked the beginning of money as we know it today.

The Origins of MONEY

ISBN: 978-1-897457-04-7

Remembering Facts and Making Assumptions

A.   Answer the following questions based on the reading passage.

1.   Name four methods of payment we can use today.

a. _____   b. _____

c. _____   d. _____

2.   What does bartering mean?

_____

3.   Make a list of things that were used as currency in ancient times.

a. _____   b. _____

c. _____   d. _____

4.   Why was the use of bronze miniatures a clever way to make a purchase?

_____

_____

5.   Why do you think that animals were such a popular form of currency?

_____

_____

6.   Why was the bartering system not always fair?

_____

_____

Your Opinion

B.   What skills would you need to possess to make you good at bartering?

1. _____

2. _____

3. _____

ISBN: 978-1-897457-04-7

Rules of Capitalization

- Here are some rules to remember:

1. Use capitals at the beginning of sentences and questions.
2. Use capitals for all proper names and titles.
3. Use capitals for book and poem titles.
4. Use capitals for months of the year and special days.
5. Use capitals for brand names, company names, and religious terms.
6. Use capitals for names of countries, cities, lakes, rivers, and regions.

C. **In the following passage, there are numerous words that should be capitalized. Change the small letters to capitals where necessary.**

In fact, there are 39 capitals missing. Can you find them?

in the month of june, professor smith took jake and jordan on a fishing trip up to moon river in the muskoka area of northern ontario. the drive from toronto took three hours but they stopped for lunch at mcdonald's. because the drive was so long, jordan brought his book entitled the best way to catch fish. he thought this book might help him learn how to fish. he was going to use the special fish hook that he received for a birthday gift in may. it was made by acme fishing gear company located in montreal. when they arrived, they passed the old st. luke's church down the road from the river. working outside the church was pastor rodgers, who also likes to fish. he waved at them as they went by.

ISBN: 978-1-897457-04-7

Haiku Poetry

- **Haiku Poetry** is a non-rhyming Japanese poem popular in the 19th century. It often dealt with nature as a theme.

- Haiku poetry consists of three lines with 5, 7, and 5 syllables in each line in that order.

  Example: Sun / surf / sand / and / sea   5 syllables

  Sail / boats / drift / ing / by / the /shore   7 syllables

  South / sea / wind / blow / ing   5 syllables

  The syllable breaks have been marked in the above poem. Notice that the poem is a collection of images (word pictures).

- Alliteration: **Alliteration** occurs when consecutive words begin with the same letter. In the poem above, there is sun, surf, sand, sea – all of which begin with the letter "s". Alliteration gives a poem a smooth rhythm and helps connect descriptive words and images.

D. Compose two Haiku poems. You may choose from the following topics or create your own. Try to use as many descriptive words as you can.

Topics:	The Storm	Summer Morning
	Winter Night	Birds in Flight
	The Lion's Den	Children Playing

Title: _____

_____

_____

_____

Title: _____

_____

_____

_____

ISBN: 978-1-897457-04-7

The interest in reaching the Far East through a northern passage was very high in Europe. The Spanish had <u>established</u> a <u>foothold</u> in South America and Mexico. The French and English, always <u>rivals</u>, were competing to <u>discover</u> a northern passage that would lead to China.

New France –
the Beginning Of Canada (1)

Francis I, king of France, selected Jacques Cartier to lead a voyage on a similar <u>route</u> to that taken by John Cabot in 1497. Cartier left France in 1534 with 2 ships and 60 men. In less than three weeks, he had crossed the Atlantic and reached Newfoundland. He <u>explored</u> the surrounding area known today as Prince Edward Island and New Brunswick. He erected a flag on Gaspé Peninsula and claimed the land for France. Cartier <u>convinced</u> an Indian chief named Donnaconna to allow him to take his two sons back to France in order to <u>impress</u> the king.

When he returned to France, Cartier was considered a hero. The king was so pleased with his efforts that he allowed for a second voyage. In 1535, Cartier set sail again with 3 ships and 110 men. When they reached the Gulf of St. Lawrence, the Indians returning with him led Cartier to the St. Lawrence River. Impressed by the size of the river, Cartier thought that the St. Lawrence River might lead to a passage to the East.

Continuing west down the St. Lawrence River, Cartier reached what is today Montreal. He named the village Mount Réal (Royal Mountain) in honour of the height of the mountain in the village. This was as far as Cartier could go because a short distance up the river, he came across rapids that were <u>impassable</u>. Cartier was forced to spend the winter there. He and his men were not prepared for the Canadian winter. They suffered <u>severe</u> cold, a <u>shortage</u> of food and supplies, and the <u>onset</u> of scurvy.

ISBN 978-1-897457-04-7

Examining Facts

A. Place "T" for true statements and "F" for false ones.

1. Europeans wanted a northern route to the East. _____

2. The Spanish had settlements in South America. _____

3. Cartier's route was different from Cabot's. _____

4. Francis I was king of France in 1534. _____

5. Cartier made it to Newfoundland in less than three weeks. _____

6. Cartier explored the area around P.E.I. and New Brunswick. _____

7. On his first voyage, Cartier left France with 200 men. _____

8. Cartier brought Indians back to France to impress the king. _____

9. Cartier took the sons of Donnaconna back to France. _____

10. Cartier was not interested in the St. Lawrence River. _____

11. Cartier visited a village which today is Montreal. _____

12. Cartier's voyage was stopped because of rapids. _____

B. Complete the chart to compare Cartier's two voyages.

		1st Voyage	2nd Voyage
1.	Date		
2.	Number of Ships and Men in the Crew		
3.	Important Accomplishments		

ISBN: 978-1-897457-04-7

Punctuation: Commas and Quotation Marks

- Place **Quotation Marks** ("...") around the exact words spoken by a person.

  Example 1: Paul said, "I am going home now."
  Note: a comma is placed after the word "said" but not before it.

  Example 2: He said, "Good morning." Note: a comma is placed after "said".
  "Good morning," he said. Note: a comma is placed after "morning".

- Place a **Comma** between words in a series.

  Example 3: I like to eat potatoes, tomatoes, carrots, and beans.

- Special Note: Place a capital at the beginning of a quotation.

C. Punctuate the following sentences where necessary.

1. She screamed Look out

2. The teacher said Tonight for homework you have Math Science and Spelling

3. He played baseball soccer basketball and hockey

4. Let's go swimming said Janet to her friends

5. Linda yelled Is anyone there

Quotation marks are used to show people speaking or a dialogue. Another way of writing a dialogue is to list the speakers, each followed by a colon, and their speech. You do not need quotation marks in this case.

Example: John: How are you today, Paul?
Paul: I'm fine. How are you?

D. Write a conversation between you and a friend. Place the speaker's name before the colon.

_____ : _____

_____ : _____

_____ : _____

_____ : _____

ISBN: 978-1-897457-04-7

New Words in Context

- We can determine the meaning of a word by the idea behind the sentence in which it appears.

E.   Solve the crossword puzzles for the underlined words in the passage.

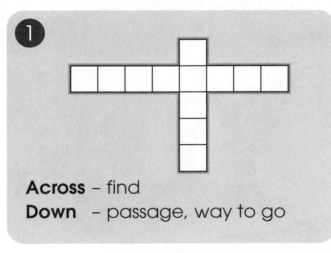

1
Across – find
Down – passage, way to go

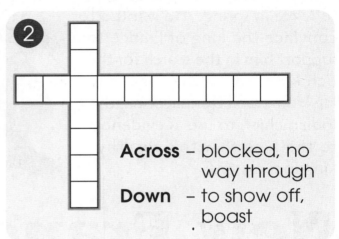

2
Across – blocked, no way through
Down – to show off, boast

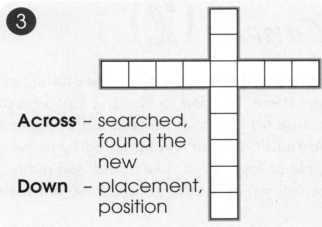

3
Across – searched, found the new
Down – placement, position

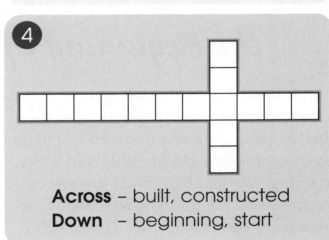

4
Across – built, constructed
Down – beginning, start

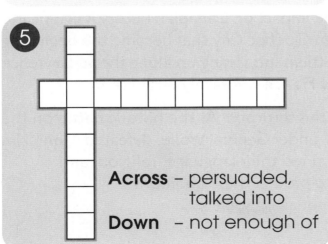

5
Across – persuaded, talked into
Down – not enough of

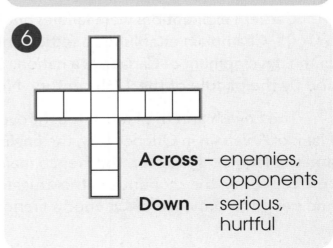

6
Across – enemies, opponents
Down – serious, hurtful

ISBN: 978-1-897457-04-7

After the <u>miserable</u> winter of 1535, twenty-five of Cartier's men had died. Cartier <u>prepared</u> to leave in spring. He wanted to convince the king of France to support him in the search for the rich kingdom of the Saguenay. He kidnapped Donnaconna, the Indian chief, to use as evidence to the king that this wealthy kingdom existed.

New France –
the Beginning Of Canada (2)

In 1541, Cartier set sail again with five ships and a thousand <u>settlers</u>. He established a settlement at present day Québec City. From there, he tried to find the kingdom of the Saguenay. He was doomed to <u>failure</u> because no kingdom existed. Once again a harsh winter brought <u>hardship</u> and illness. Worse still, Cartier was <u>attacked</u> by natives. In spring, Cartier abandoned the settlement. He brought back quartz and iron pyrites, minerals that he <u>thought</u> were valuable. Also known as "Fool's gold", these minerals were worthless.

Cartier's explorations were failures but the impact on Canadian history is significant. In 1608, Champlain established a settlement in Québec City that became the beginning of the <u>development</u> of Canada as a nation. Settlements sprang up along the St. Lawrence and by the middle of the 17th century, New France was firmly established.

The English and the French <u>fought</u> over this territory. At the historic battle on the Plains of Abraham in Québec City, the English, under General Wolfe, defeated Montcalm and the French. However, the French maintained their language, religion, and culture. Today, they continue in the struggle to protect these traditions and keep the province of Quebec a French-speaking society.

ISBN: 978-1-897457-04-7

Fact or Opinion

- A **Fact** is an exact statement given in the story. An **Opinion** is your personal point of view based on what you have read.

A. **Place "F" for fact or "O" for opinion for each statement in the space provided.**

1. Canadian winters can be harsh. _____

2. It is easier to travel in spring. _____

3. 25 of Cartier's men died. _____

4. Cartier thought there were riches in the Saguenay. _____

5. Cartier was cruel to Donnaconna. _____

6. Cartier wanted to prove to the king that there were riches in the Saguenay region. _____

7. Cartier was anxious to build a settlement. _____

8. There were no riches in the Saguenay region. _____

9. Quartz and iron pyrites could be used as jewelry. _____

B. **In your opinion, was Cartier a success or a failure? Make a list of his successes and his failures in the chart below.**

Accomplishments	Failures/Hardships
1.	1.
2.	2.
3.	3.

C. **What natural wealth was there in Canada that Cartier overlooked?**

_____

_____

ISBN: 978-1-897457-04-7

Problem Sentences

- **Sentence Fragments**: *a sentence fragment is an incomplete sentence.*

  Example: *When I walk home from school...*
  This fragment needs more information for it to make sense.

  If you add "I see my friends on the way", then you would have:
  When I walk home from school, I see my friends on the way.

D. Correct the following sentence fragments by adding the necessary information.

1. During my lunch hour, _____ .

2. After it stopped raining, _____ .

3. _____ because the teacher asked.

4. If it isn't too late, _____ .

5. While I am watching television, _____ .

Combining Sentences

- *Some sentences are too short. They are better when combined with another sentence that refers to the same topic.*

  Example: It was Saturday morning. I woke up late.

  Could become: It was Saturday morning and I woke up late. or
  This Saturday morning, I woke up late.

E. Combine the following short sentences.

Don't forget to use conjunctions.

1. Carol called on Julie. Julie was not home.

   _____

2. Friday is a holiday. There is no school.

   _____

3. My teacher is nice. Mrs. Smith is my teacher. She teaches grade four.

   _____

4. Philip had a doctor's appointment. It was on Tuesday.

   _____

ISBN: 978-1-897457-04-7

Word Builder Crossword Puzzles

F. **Each puzzle contains three root words for the underlined words in the reading passage. Use the clues to help you solve the puzzles.**

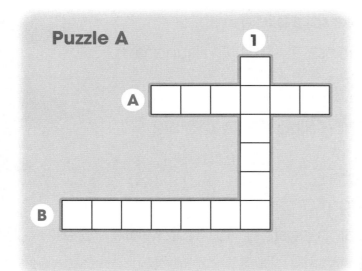

Puzzle A

Across – A. sadness
B. get ready

Down – 1. make ready, calm, rest

Puzzle B

Across – A. form an idea
B. build, make, form

Down – 1. firm, tough, difficult

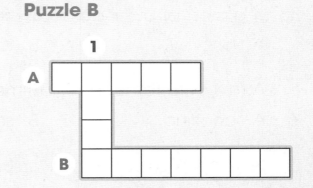

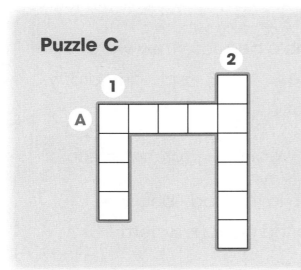

Puzzle C

Across – A. battle

Down – 1. not win
2. charge

ISBN: 978-1-897457-04-7

Multiple Choice

A. Circle the correct answer for each of the statements from the reading passages.

1. The number of Harry Potter books sold is in the

   A. thousands.   B. millions.   C. hundreds.

2. Before writing her books, J.K. Rowling was

   A. very wealthy.   B. a struggling single mother.

   C. a housewife.

3. Pioneer children got their toys from

   A. making their own.   B. trading posts.   C. hardware stores.

4. The most popular game of pioneer times across Canada was

   A. hockey.   B. lacrosse.   C. horseshoe pitching.

5. A favourite father-son pastime in pioneer times was

   A. cooking.   B. sewing.   C. fishing.

6. When pioneer children weren't playing, they were

   A. doing chores.   B. sleeping.   C. watching television.

7. Early castles were not very comfortable because they were

   A. high on a hill.   B. too large.   C. cold and drafty.

8. The main purpose of a castle was

   A. to hold big parties. B. to show wealth. C. for protection.

9. The brain is the most important organ in the body because

   A. it is large.   B. it links to the nervous system.

   C. it helps us think.

ISBN: 978-1-897457-04-7

10. The human brain stops growing when we are about

    A. 6 years old.   B. 18 years old.   C. 35 years old.

11. The human brain, when it is fully developed, weighs about

    A. 10 kg.   B. 25 kg.   C. 3 kg.

12. The Inca Empire ended when their territory was taken over by

    A. the French.   B. the Spanish.   C. the Portuguese.

13. The Inca built their cities on

    A. highlands.   B. flatlands.   C. cliffs.

14. Before the use of money, deals were made by

    A. guessing.   B. bartering.   C. arguing.

15. For trade in China, people used

    A. bronze miniatures.   B. snakeskin.   C. furs.

16. Cartier returned to France with

    A. riches.   B. gold and jewels.   C. an Indian chief.

17. Cartier thought that riches lay in

    A. the Saguenay Region.   B. the St. Lawrence River.

    C. Montreal.

18. Cartier's men suffered from a disease called

    A. influenza.   B. scurvy.   C. smallpox.

19. Cartier attempted to build a settlement at present day

    A. Toronto.   B. Montreal.   C. Québec City.

20. In 1608, a settlement in Quebec was established by

    A. King Francis I.   B. John Cabot.   C. Champlain.

 **Prepositions**

B.   Add a suitable preposition in the space provided.

1.   He hid _____ the table.   (under, through, inside)

2.   She sunbathed _____ the backyard.   (under, into, in)

3.   The dog ran _____ the yard.   (around, between, throughout)

4.   The boat sailed _____ the river.   (into, down, between)

 Phrases and Clauses

C.   Write "P" if the underlined words are phrases or "C" if they are clauses.

1.   <u>The purse on the bench</u> belonged to the old lady.   _____

2.   I didn't go to Matt's party <u>because I was ill</u>.   _____

3.   <u>Whenever they are free</u>, they play video games.   _____

4.   The man <u>with a moustache on his face</u> is the manager.   _____

 Adjective and Adverb Phrases

D.   State whether the underlined words represent an adjective or an adverb phrase. Place ADJ or ADV in the space.

A phrase is a group of words introduced by a preposition that describes either a verb or a noun.

1.   Go <u>into the garage</u> and get the lawn mower.   _____

2.   The players <u>on the junior team</u> practise every day.   _____

3.   The girls <u>in the class</u> sat <u>in the front</u>.   _____

4.   <u>In the evening</u>, they watched a movie.   _____

5.   The seat <u>in the front</u> cost much more money.   _____

ISBN: 978-1-897457-04-7

Conjunctions

Conjunctions join other words, phrases, or main ideas in a sentence.

E. **Underline the conjunctions in the following sentences.**

1. It may taste bad but it's good for you.

2. She will not be late if she leaves on time.

3. Either Joe or Paul will be captain of the team.

4. It was overcast although the forecast was for sunny weather.

Capitalization and Punctuation

F. **Correct the missing capitals in each sentence. Add proper punctuation.**

1. mr. smith asked john to meet him at lions stadium

2. she said could someone please assist me

3. lauren and kara read a judy blume story

4. peaches plums pears and nectarines are expensive in winter

5. he shouted let me in it's cold outside

Types of Sentences

G. **State whether the following sentences are declarative, imperative, interrogative, or exclamatory and punctuate them accordingly.**

1. Get up now _____

2. Who will help with the work _____

3. Wow _____

4. This is the main street in town _____

ISBN: 978-1-897457-04-7

New Words from the Reading Passages

H. Match the words from the passages with the definitions.

1.	vital	_____	A.	searched, looked into
2.	responsibility	_____	B.	imaginative
3.	amazing	_____	C.	serious, dangerous
4.	complex	_____	D.	unknown
5.	creative	_____	E.	enemies
6.	mystery	_____	F.	important
7.	rivals	_____	G.	duty
8.	explored	_____	H.	not enough
9.	severe	_____	I.	complicated, numerous
10.	shortage	_____	J.	surprising, unbelievable

I. Complete the sentences with the correct form of the given words.

1. Yesterday Paul (laugh) _____ when he heard the joke.

2. The sun shone on the (beauty) _____ flowers.

3. The bird was (chirp) _____ loudly.

4. Crossing the road can be (danger) _____ .

5. She was (perform) _____ in the school play.

6. They lived (happy) _____ ever after.

7. He made a (donate) _____ to the charity.

8. Being on time proved that she was (rely) _____ .

ISBN: 978-1-897457-04-7

9. The puppy was very (life) _____ .

10. The children were (terrify) _____ by the scary movie.

Forming New Words

J. Choose the proper prefix for each of the following words.

1. sincere   in, un   : _____

2. direct   in, de   : _____

3. patient   un, im   : _____

4. belief   dis, un   : _____

5. known   non, un   : _____

6. proper   un, im   : _____

7. behave   mis, dis   : _____

8. certain   dis, un   : _____

9. believable   un, im   : _____

Plurals

K. Write the proper plural form of the following words.

1. hero		2. army	
3. city		4. lady	
5. life		6. leaf	
7. half		8. tomato	
9. goose		10. mouse	

ISBN: 978-1-897457-04-7

ISBN: 978-1-897457-04-7

Outside

Inside

ISBN: 978-1-897457-04-7

Subjects

The **subject** of a verb is the person or thing that performs the action. It can be a noun or a pronoun.

Examples: <u>Ken</u> is reading the school yearbook.
    <u>It</u> is very cute.

In the first sentence, "Ken" is the subject who does the action "reading".
In the second sentence, "it" is the subject being described.

A. Underline the subject of each sentence.

1. Joe enjoys scuba diving.

2. The mouse ran off quickly.

3. The tallest girl in the class is Amy.

4. They hid the eggs in the woods.

5. He was on the football team last year.

6. Helen's goal is winning the gold medal in the singing contest.

B. Complete the sentences with suitable subjects.

1. _____ put her money in the bank.

2. _____ was unbelievable.

3. _____ is important to the environment.

4. _____ were fighting on the street.

5. _____ prefers Italian food.

ISBN: 978-1-897457-04-7

Objects

The **object** of a verb is the person or thing that receives the action of the verb. It can be a noun or a pronoun.

Examples: Mom bought <u>a picture</u> yesterday.
The old lady asked <u>me</u> for help.

C. Circle the correct objects.

1. The teacher took English / the students to the farm.

2. Can you sign your name / the ball on my T-shirt?

3. I like music / sing very much.

4. Dad washed his it / car with the new cleanser.

5. The cat is chasing the mouse / kitchen .

D. Fill in the blanks with the given words.

fish	me	camera	bikes	tent
photos	stars	sandwiches		

Last weekend, Dad took 1._____ camping. We set up our 2._____ near the lake. Then we rode our 3._____ on the nearby trails. I brought my 4._____ with me and took lots of 5._____ . We had 6._____ for lunch. Then we went fishing. Dad caught a few 7._____ but I caught none. We stayed up late to watch the 8._____ . We were enchanted by the beautiful night sky.

> ### Direct Objects
>
> A **direct object** is the noun or pronoun that receives the action of the verb.
>
> *Example*:   I wash <u>the dishes</u>.
>
> Some sentences carry no objects.
>
> *Example*:   The baby cried.

E.   Underline the direct objects in the passage below.

My sister likes gardening. She has grown many plants in the backyard. They include fruit trees, flowers, and herbs. She waters the plants every day. Her flowers are in different colours: red, pink, white, and yellow. Sometimes, she cuts some flowers and places them in the dining room. They make the room look beautiful. They smell sweet, too.

F.   Complete the sentences with suitable direct objects.

1.   Miss Key punished _____ .

2.   Jackson has painted _____ .

3.   The children wrapped _____ .

4.   Charles broke _____ .

5.   The snake ate _____ .

ISBN: 978-1-897457-04-7

Indirect Objects

An **indirect object** is the noun or pronoun to whom or to what the verb is directed.

Example: Fred is building <u>Bobby</u> a house.

In this sentence, "Bobby" is the indirect object and "house" is the direct object.

G. Write "D" if the underlined words are direct objects and "I" for indirect objects.

1. Dad bought <u>a new digital camera</u> for Mom.   _____

2. Please show <u>me</u> your picture.   _____

3. Janice told them <u>the truth</u>.   _____

4. Can you give <u>him</u> a call tomorrow?   _____

5. Come on! Pass <u>me</u> the ball.   _____

6. The nurse handed the dentist <u>the tool</u>.   _____

H. Write sentences using the given words as indirect objects.

1. the policeman

_____

2. her

_____

3. his dog

_____

4. the school

_____

ISBN: 978-1-897457-04-7

unit 2 Pronouns

A. Circle the correct pronouns.

Bonnie and Jennifer are in my class.

1. She / They are my best friends. 2. We / Us like skipping very much and I enjoy playing with 3. they / them . Bonnie is the best player. 4. He / She always wins. I can never beat 5. she / her .

Every year, Mom makes Halloween costumes for 6. we / us . This year, she made a hat and a cloak for 7. I / me . 8. I / Me will dress like a witch and take a broom with me. 9. She / Her made a tiger costume for my younger brother. 10. It / He really fits 11. it / him because 12. he / she always acts like a tiger. 13. We / Us will go around in our neighbourhood to get candies.

ISBN: 978-1-897457-04-7

Possessive Pronouns

A **possessive pronoun** shows ownership or relationship. It is not followed by a noun.

Possessive pronouns: mine, yours, ours, theirs, his, hers

Example: I've cleaned my stick.
Have you cleaned <u>yours</u>?

"Yours" is a possessive pronoun referring to "your stick". Note that there is no need to put "stick" after "yours".

B. Rewrite the sentences with possessive pronouns.

Example: This is my cheese.
This cheese is mine.

1. This is Jerry's present.

   _____

2. These are your cards.

   _____

3. This is my parents' bed.

   _____

4. That is Mary's lunch box.

   _____

5. These are my photo albums.

   _____

6. This is Pansy and my secret.

   _____

ISBN: 978-1-897457-04-7

Interrogative Pronouns

An **interrogative pronoun** asks a question. "Who", "what", "which", "whose", and "whom" are interrogative pronouns.

Examples: <u>What</u> did you have for dinner?
<u>Whose</u> are these? Are they Ivan's?

C. Fill in the blanks with appropriate interrogative pronouns.

1. _____ should I pick? They all look yummy.

2. To _____ did you talk?

3. _____ is wrong with your car?

4. _____ is this? Is it yours?

5. _____ built this sandcastle?

6. _____ wants to come with me?

7. _____ do you like, the cake or the pie?

D. Check if the underlined interrogative pronouns are correct. If not, write the correct ones on the lines.

1. <u>Whose</u> will you choose from this menu?   _____

2. <u>Who</u> has he done to make you angry?   _____

3. With <u>which</u> would you like to dance?   _____

4. <u>Which</u> is heavier, a bike or a car?   _____

5. <u>Who</u> won the gold medal in the long jump?   _____

6. <u>What</u> brought this birthday cake?   _____

7. I found this key. <u>Whose</u> is it?   _____

ISBN: 978-1-897457-04-7

E. Unscramble the words to form questions.

1. boot   my   put   who   here

   _____

2. the   find   box   he   what   did   in

   _____

3. these   whose   are

   _____

4. take   I   which   should

   _____

5. picture   scary   took   who   this

   _____

6. whom   concert   to   you   will   the   take

   _____

7. whose   highest   is   one   the

   _____

8. chosen   which   you   have

   _____

F. Complete the following questions.

1. Who _____ ?

2. What _____ ?

3. Which _____ ?

4. Whose _____ ?

5. Whom _____ ?

ISBN: 978-1-897457-04-7

> ### Simple Present Tense
>
> Verbs can be in different tenses. The **simple present tense** talks about facts, present actions, and habitual actions. Most present tense verbs for third person singular subjects are formed by adding "s" or "es" to the base form.
>
> *Example*:   Eric <u>rides</u> a bike to school.

A. Underline the simple present tense verbs in the passage below.

Mom likes going out for dinner. She says it gives her a break from cooking. On Fridays, Dad takes her to her favourite restaurant. Mom tries something new each week but Dad orders pasta every time. Dad likes eating there, too. He says the only part he hates is when it is time to pay! When they go, a neighbour watches my sister and me. We play games and eat pizza.

B. Fill in the blanks with the correct simple present tense form of the given verbs.

1. We _____ milkshakes.
   (drink)

2. She _____ the dishes.
   (wash)

3. Krista _____ for her History test.
   (study)

4. Canada _____ a big country.
   (be)

5. It _____ very cold outside.
   (feel)

ISBN: 978-1-897457-04-7

Simple Past Tense

The **simple past tense** talks about past actions. Most past tense verbs are formed by adding "d" or "ed" to the base form.

Example: We <u>helped</u> Mom do the housework this morning.

Some past tense verbs have irregular endings.

Example: I <u>caught</u> a fish yesterday.

C. Circle the verbs that are in the simple past tense.

Yesterday, Kara   *1.* played / plays   with Michelle during recess. They   *2.* decide / decided   to play catch. Joshua *3.* notices / noticed   them playing. He *4.* asked / asks   if he could play, too. Joshua   *5.* said / says   he   *6.* used / uses to play catch a lot when he   *7.* lives / lived in Hawaii. The three   *8.* kept / keep playing until the bell   *9.* rang / rings   .

D. Fill in the blank with the simple past tense of the given verb.

1. John (write) _____ a story and (give) _____ it to me.

2. She (speak) _____ too loudly in the library.

3. The kettle (whistle) _____ when the water (boil) _____ .

4. It (take) _____ us three hours to get to the cottage.

5. Raindrops (fall) _____ on my head while I (sit) _____ and (wait) _____ .

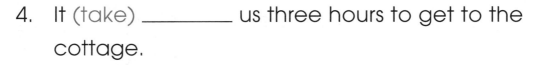

Simple Future Tense

The **simple future tense** talks about future actions. The verb is formed by adding "will" before the base form.

Example: Jane <u>will sing</u> a song.

E. **Check if the verbs are in the simple future tense. If not, write the verbs in simple future tense on the lines.**

1. Dad will bring home a treat for us.   _____

2. Aunt Trudy made a pot of tea.   _____

3. I'll come home in about an hour.   _____

4. Annie helped me with my homework.   _____

5. Will you give me the recipe?   _____

6. The zoo will be a lot of fun!   _____

7. Grandpa took me fishing.   _____

F. **Fill in the blanks with the correct verbs in the simple future tense.**

come   go   be   see   bake

1. I _____ many clowns at the circus.

2. The sun _____ out tomorrow.

3. Lindsay _____ an apple pie.

4. The soccer game _____ exciting.

5. The Wilson family _____ to Italy next week.

ISBN: 978-1-897457-04-7

G. Check the correct boxes to show if the sentences are in the present, past, or future tense.

	Present	Past	Future

1. Gary returned the books to the library.

2. Maria will go to the musical tonight.

3. Mom grows a lot of flowers every summer.

4. The windows are windproof.

5. Don didn't finish his homework in time.

6. Will you tell me the truth?

7. We watched the sun set.

8. Is this watermelon sweet?

9. I'll show you the way.

H. Rewrite the sentences. Change the underlined verbs to the correct tenses.

1. Sam <u>win</u> the gold medal in the long jump.

_____

2. It <u>be</u> rainy tomorrow.

_____

3. The hurricane <u>bring</u> a lot of rain last week.

_____

4. Every winter, my brother and I <u>made</u> a snowman.

_____

5. The Parliament Buildings <u>be</u> in Ottawa.

_____

ISBN: 978-1-897457-04-7

unit 4 Adjectives

Comparative Adjectives

A **comparative adjective** compares two nouns. For adjectives with one syllable, the comparative form is formed by adding "er". For adjectives with two or more syllables, add "more" before the original adjective.

Example: The roses are <u>taller</u> than the tulips but the tulips are <u>more beautiful</u>.

Some adjectives have irregular comparative forms.

Example: The weather today is <u>better</u> than yesterday's.

A. Write the comparative form of the adjectives on the lines.

1. comfortable _____

2. new _____

3. cheap _____

4. difficult _____

5. easy _____

6. bright _____

B. Fill in the blanks with the comparative form of the given adjectives and any other necessary words.

1. Walking uphill is (tiring) _____ going downhill.

2. Sandra is (capable) _____ Peggy.

3. I am (strong) _____ you.

4. Danielle is (slim) _____ her sister.

5. This book is (interesting) _____ that book.

ISBN: 978-1-897457-04-7

Superlative Adjectives

A **superlative adjective** compares three or more nouns. For adjectives with one syllable, the superlative form is formed by adding "est". For adjectives with two or more syllables, add "most" before the original adjective.

Example: Tim is the <u>fastest</u> runner in his class. He is also the <u>most hard-working</u> student.

Some adjectives have irregular superlative forms.

Example: Daisy thinks that she is the <u>best</u> among her friends.

C. Complete the chart.

	Original	Comparative	Superlative
1.	small		
2.	bad		
3.			most famous
4.	happy		
5.		more colourful	
6.	less		

D. Fill in the blanks with the superlative form of the given adjectives and any other necessary words.

1. The coat I wear is (thick) _____ one I have.

2. Sasa is (old) _____ one in the litter.

3. The teddy bear was (wanted) _____ toy last year.

4. Chapter ten is (scary) _____ of all.

5. He is (active) _____ player on the team.

ISBN: 978-1-897457-04-7

Nouns as Adjectives

A noun can be used to describe another noun in the same way as an adjective.

Example: Bobo is so cute that we all treat it as our <u>family</u> member.

E. **Draw a line to join each noun in Column A to the noun it can describe in Column B.**

Column A

1. basketball   ●

2. sailing   ●

3. chocolate   ●

4. music   ●

5. radio   ●

Column B

●   room

●   program

●   sundae

●   boat

●   team

F. **Look at the pictures. Fill in the missing letters.**

1

ch___ ___ ___ ___
p___e

2

___r___ ___s___ ___ ___
b___ ___

3

___is___
b___ ___l

4

___ ___f___e___
___ ___g

5

___ ___nc___ ___
___ha___ ___ ___ ___er

ISBN: 978-1-897457-04-7

G. Write nouns that can be described by the given nouns.

1. computer _____

2. bowling _____

3. Christmas _____

4. air _____

5. leather _____

6. bus _____

7. apple _____

8. paper _____

H. Fill in the blanks with the given words.

1. The children are looking at the boat at the _____ shop.

2. Let's meet at the _____ court at noon.

3. Don't forget to put the _____ tape in.

4. The _____ clips look nice on you.

5. Dad has bought a _____ ring for Mom.

6. Our car is stuck in the _____ jam.

7. My parents held a _____ party for me.

8. Do you want to try a _____ pocket?

9. My _____ clock is not working.

10. I would like to get some _____ candy after a long day in the park.

pizza
alarm
toy
birthday
hair
video
traffic
tennis
diamond
cotton

ISBN: 978-1-897457-04-7

unit 5 Adverbs

Adverbs

An **adverb** is a word that describes a verb. Adverbs explain where, when, how, how much, or how long.

Examples:
The dog barked <u>fiercely</u>. (how)
The Watts go there <u>weekly</u>. (when)
The girl took the doll <u>away</u>. (where)
The snow seemed to fall <u>forever</u>. (how long)

A. **Complete the following sentences with these adverbs.**

later   usually   hard   carelessly
yesterday   easily   here   hardly   well

1. I'll let you have the report _____ .

2. He had an accident because he drove _____ .

3. They worked _____ to make sure that they could finish the job before noon.

4. The boys _____ play hockey at the arena on weekends.

5. Mrs. Watson left for Nova Scotia _____ .

6. The smart kid solved the problem _____ .

7. Samuel has grown so much that we _____ recognize him.

8. Would you like to come _____ for lunch?

9. The party went _____ and everyone had a great time.

ISBN: 978-1-897457-04-7

"Good" and "Well"

"Good" is an adjective that describes a noun or a pronoun.

Example: The hot dog is really <u>good</u>.

"Well" is an adverb that describes a verb.

Example: She speaks Russian <u>well</u>.

B. Complete the following sentences with "good" or "well". Circle the words that they describe.

1. We had a _____ time singing and dancing.

2. The show was really _____ .

3. He thought he did pretty _____ on the test.

4. A warm mug of chocolate made me feel _____ after shovelling the snow.

5. The teacher thinks that we have done a _____ job.

6. Pat can play the violin _____ .

7. The program went _____ as planned.

C. Write a sentence each with "hard" and "hardly" to show their difference.

"Hard" means with great effort while "hardly" means almost not.

1. hard:

2. hardly:

ISBN: 978-1-897457-04-7

Changing Adjectives to Adverbs

Most adverbs are formed by adding "ly" to an adjective.

Example: My sister and I are folding the clothes <u>neatly</u>.

For adjectives ending in "y", drop the "y" and add "ily" to form an adverb.

Example: The children were singing <u>happily</u>.

D. Underline the adverbs in the following sentences.

1. The pirate asked his man to row quickly.

2. They went into the cave cautiously.

3. This dress is specially designed for you.

4. It is awfully smelly here.

5. He is thinking seriously about the riddle.

6. They are waiting for their coach patiently.

7. Do you think you can do it easily?

8. The soldiers are standing solemnly at the entrance.

9. They planned their trip thoughtfully.

10. The lights went off suddenly.

11. Dad washed his car thoroughly.

12. He dashed past the defenseman swiftly.

E. Fill in the blanks with the given adverbs.

unfortunately	early	quickly	happily
quietly	softly	luckily	patiently

Yesterday Dad and I went fishing. We had to get up
1. _____ because fish usually stay away from the shore in
the afternoon. We waited 2. _____ and 3. _____ for
the fish. "Hey Dad, I can feel something moving," I told Dad
4. _____ . Dad helped me pull my line 5. _____ .
6. _____ , it was a very small fish and we threw it back into
the water. We stayed there for four hours. 7. _____ , we
did catch some fish. We went home 8. _____ .

F. Change the following adjectives to adverbs.

1. surprising _____   2. merry _____

3. terrible _____   4. anxious _____

5. clear _____   6. greedy _____

G. Write sentences using the adverbs formed in (F).

1. _____

2. _____

3. _____

4. _____

5. _____

6. _____

ISBN: 978-1-897457-04-7

unit 6 Conjunctions

> ### Conjunctions
>
> **Conjunctions** are joining words. They are used to join a word to another word, or a sentence to another sentence.
>
> *Examples*: Matt likes popsicles <u>and</u> ice cream.
> You may have an ice cream <u>or</u> a popsicle <u>but</u> not both.
> We are leaving for Calgary <u>but</u> Dad has to stay behind.

A. Complete the following sentences with suitable conjunctions.

1. The Fall Fair has many displays _____ thrilling rides.

2. Most of the children wanted an outing _____ Mrs. Baker suggested a pizza party.

3. Was he born on the eighth _____ the eighteenth?

4. They bought juice, vegetables, fruits, _____ bread.

5. Both Cindy _____ Wilfred represent our class.

6. He wants to be a professional baseball player _____ he is not good at batting _____ pitching.

7. Which painting is yours, this one _____ that one?

8. I can't work on the sums _____ watch TV at the same time.

9. The pumpkin is a bright orange colour _____ weighs more than 200 kilograms.

ISBN: 978-1-897457-04-7

B. Combine the sentence pairs into one sentence using "and", "but", or "or".

Example: The pony eats oats. The pony eats hay.
The pony eats oats and hay.

1. Owls sleep during the day and hunt at night.
    Bats sleep during the day and hunt at night.

    _____

    _____

2. The days are hot in the summer.
    The days are cold in the winter.

    _____

    _____

3. We can take the midnight flight.
    We can take the morning flight the next day.

    _____

    _____

4. Greg doesn't like to eat spinach.
    Greg likes to eat broccoli.

    _____

    _____

5. You can go there to apply in person.
    You can fax the form to them.

    _____

    _____

ISBN: 978-1-897457-04-7

"Before" and "After"

"**Before**" and "**after**" link sentences together as **conjunctions**. They can be used to begin, or placed in the middle of, a sentence.

Examples: I packed my clothes. Then I went swimming.
<u>After</u> I packed my clothes, I went swimming.
I went swimming <u>after</u> I packed my clothes.
<u>Before</u> I went swimming, I packed my clothes.
I packed my clothes <u>before</u> I went swimming.

Note that when "before" or "after" is used to begin a sentence, a comma is needed between the clauses.

C. Fill in the blanks with "before" or "after".

1. Don't forget to put a stamp on _____ you post the letter.

2. I always put the toys back in the box _____ I finish playing.

3. _____ you go to bed, set the alarm clock.

4. We helped Mom clean up _____ the guests left.

5. Give it to the librarian _____ you fill out the form.

6. They pray _____ they eat.

7. _____ we got on the bus, we showed the transfer tickets to the bus driver.

8. _____ I have touched up the photos, I will send them to you.

9. _____ we went on board, we had to go through security check.

Security Check

D. Read the recipe. Complete the sentences with "before" or "after" and with the help of the given words.

Rice Krispy Treats

6 cups Rice Krispies

200 grams butter

4 cups marshmallows

1 cup peanut butter

- Melt butter, marshmallows, and peanut butter over low heat in a large pan.
- Remove from heat and stir in Rice Krispies.
- Spread into a large buttered flat pan.
- Pat down with buttered hands.
- Cool and cut into squares.

1. _____ , have all the ingredients on hand. (get started)

2. _____ , marshmallows, and peanut butter, remove the pan from heat. (melt butter)

3. _____ , spread the mixture into a large buttered flat pan. (in stir Rice Krispies)

4. Butter your hands _____ . (pat down mixture)

5. Let it cool for half an hour _____ . (squares cut into it)

A. Read the story. Circle the subject of each sentence.

Hop and Scotch are two rabbits who live in a forest. There are lots of leaves and grasses to eat there, but sometimes the rabbits want to eat something more interesting. They discovered a garden outside the forest. It belongs to a farmer. Sometimes they will go there to munch on the delicious vegetables that grow there.

It is early in the morning and Hop and Scotch have just woken up. They are both extremely hungry. Scotch says, "Hop, I'd like to have some vegetables today. I think we should go to the garden for a treat."

"I like your idea," says Hop. "It is a beautiful day and the perfect weather to make the trip."

Scotch is a competitive rabbit. "I think that we should have a race," he says.

Hop is not very competitive but thinks this could make the trip a bit more fun. "Sure!" he says. Off they go! Both Hop and Scotch are very fast. It is anyone's guess who will win this race.

ISBN: 978-1-897457-04-7

B. Read these sentences from the story. Write who or what the underlined pronouns refer to.

1. <u>It</u> belongs to a farmer. _____

2. <u>They</u> are both extremely hungry. _____

3. <u>I</u>'d like to have some vegetables today. _____

4. <u>I</u> like your idea. _____

5. I think that <u>we</u> should have a race. _____

6. "Sure!" <u>he</u> says. _____

C. Fill in each blank with the correct object from the list.

> forest   garden   farmer   vegetables   lettuce

1. Hop and Scotch like all kinds of _____ .

2. Scotch likes to eat _____ more than the other vegetables.

3. Hop and Scotch discovered the _____ not too long ago.

4. They live in the _____ .

5. The rabbits don't like the _____ because he chases them away.

ISBN: 978-1-897457-04-7

D. Fill in the blanks with the correct simple present form of the given verbs.

Before they have gone very far, they (meet) 1._____ Buzzer, a bumblebee. "Move it, Buzzer!" says Scotch. "We (be) 2._____ in the middle of a race!"

"I (be) 3._____ sorry to bother you, but I need some help. I am having trouble finding some flowers and I (need) 4._____ nectar to feed my family," says Buzzer.

"What a shame," says Scotch, "but we are hungry, too. Good luck!" says Scotch before he (hop) 5._____ away.

"I will help you," (say) 6._____ Hop. Together, Buzzer and Hop are able to find a few flowers hidden behind some rocks.

E. Rewrite each sentence by changing the underlined verb to the given tense.

1. Buzzer <u>was</u> a bumblebee. (simple present tense)

   _____

2. Hop <u>helps</u> Buzzer. (simple past tense)

   _____

3. Buzzer and Hop <u>found</u> the flowers. (simple future tense)

   _____

4. Scotch <u>races</u> anyone willing to race him. (simple future tense)

   _____

ISBN: 978-1-897457-04-7

F. Write the correct comparative adjectives to complete the sentences.

1. Scotch is (competitive) _____ than Hop.

2. Hop is (friendly) _____ than Scotch.

3. Scotch wants to find out if he is (fast) _____ than Hop.

4. Buzzer is (small) _____ than the rabbits.

5. The flowers are (beautiful) _____ than Hop and Buzzer have imagined.

6. The vegetables in the garden are (tasty) _____ than the leaves in the forest.

G. Rewrite the sentences. Change the adjectives to superlative adjectives.

1. Scotch is greedy compared to the rest of the animals in the forest.

   _____

2. Lettuce is a popular vegetable in the garden.

   _____

3. Of all of the friends in the forest, Buzzer and Hop are great friends.

   _____

4. There are many different ways to get to the garden, but Hop and Scotch want a fast way.

   _____

ISBN: 978-1-897457-04-7

H. Change the adjectives to adverbs and fill in the blanks.

quick	hard	sudden	fast	kind	happy

"Thank you for helping me find the flowers," says Buzzer. "We worked 1._____. Since you've 2._____ helped me, I will 3._____ help you. I know a shortcut to get to the garden."

Buzzer and Hop 4._____ catch up to Scotch. "How did you get here so 5._____ ?" asks a surprised Scotch.

"My friend helped me," says Hop. The three continue on their way. As they race along, they 6._____ hear a voice.

I. Write sentences using the adverbs in (H).

1. _____

2. _____

3. _____

4. _____

5. _____

6. _____

ISBN: 978-1-897457-04-7

J. Underline the conjunctions in the passage.

"Yoo-hoo!" calls the voice. It is Hop's friend, Flutter the Robin. "I am having a hard time finding worms. Would you be able to help me or are you in a hurry?"

"Of course we will!" say Hop and Buzzer after they notice that Scotch has already left.

The three friends look for worms and discuss their lives. "There are not a lot of worms here but we will make do with whatever we've got," says Flutter before he tucks the worms away. "Where are you two going?" Hop tells Flutter about the race. "Scotch might be farther ahead but I know a faster way to get to that garden," he says.

K. Fill in the blanks with the correct conjunctions.

> **but   after   and   before**

1. The friends discuss what they will do _____ they are finished in the garden.

2. Hop wants to make it to the garden _____ Scotch gets there.

3. The friends think they will beat Scotch _____ he is already in the garden when they arrive.

4. They find Scotch with a full belly _____ a smile on his face, lying in the middle of the empty vegetable patch.

ISBN: 978-1-897457-04-7

unit 7 Sentences (1)

Subjects

A sentence contains a subject and a predicate. The **subject** of a sentence tells who or what the sentence is about. It can be a noun or a pronoun.

Example: My brother is a teacher. He teaches music.

A **compound subject** has two or more nouns or pronouns. They are joined by the conjunction "and".

Example: Brad and I slept in the same tent.

A. Underline the subjects in the passage below.

Last week, I went to a summer camp. We joined many activities such as swimming, ball games, and talent shows. My favourite activity was arts and crafts. Hats, beaded bracelets, and dream catchers were some of the things we made. I gave a bracelet to my best friend Hilda. She likes it very much and wears it all the time.

B. Complete the sentences with suitable subjects.

1. _____ are important to plants.

2. _____ attracts a lot of visitors.

3. _____ have gone for holiday.

4. _____ made me exhausted.

5. _____ is chasing the mouse.

ISBN: 978-1-897457-04-7

Predicates

The **predicate** of a sentence is the part that describes the subject. It contains a verb describing the action performed by the subject.

Example: Steven <u>sings very well</u>.

C. **Look at the picture. Complete the sentences with suitable predicates.**

1. The zoo _____ .

2. The zookeeper _____ .

3. The elephant _____ .

4. The panda _____ .

5. The tiger _____ .

6. Josh _____ .

7. Edith and I _____ .

ISBN: 978-1-897457-04-7

D. **Draw a vertical line between the subject and predicate in each sentence. Circle the compound subjects.**

1. I finished my homework.

2. Jill and I are going to the store.

3. Charlie wants an ice cream cone.

4. My mom and dad took me shopping.

5. His brown dog wagged its tail.

6. Main Street is very busy.

7. The duck and the hen became friends.

8. The noisy girls and boys talked and talked during the movie.

E. **Match the subjects and predicates to make suitable sentences. Write the letters.**

1. The big, green frog _____   **A** is knitting me a sweater.

2. My grandmother _____   **B** share our candies.

3. You _____   **C** has six strings.

4. The birds _____   **D** swallows flies.

5. We _____   **E** build nests.

6. The electric guitar _____   **F** are my best friend.

ISBN: 978-1-897457-04-7

F. Unscramble the sentences below. Then circle the subject of each sentence.

1. hamburger   tasty   I   a   ate

   _____

2. black   rode   a   Tony   horse

   _____

3. I   up   Craig   and   hiked   mountain   the

   _____

4. students   teacher   the   their   liked

   _____

5. studied   and   Daniel   together   Lily

   _____

6. Calgary   are   cities   and   Vancouver

   _____

G. Make sentences by adding subjects or predicates.

1. Lions and tigers _____ .

2. _____ made a huge mess.

3. _____ worked on a project together.

4. My aunt and uncle _____ .

5. The superhero _____ .

6. _____ found a secret passage.

7. Strawberry milkshakes _____ .

8. _____ climbed the tallest tree.

ISBN: 978-1-897457-04-7

unit 8 Sentences (2)

Subject-Verb Agreement

In a sentence, the **verb** must **agree** with the **subject**.
If the subject is singular, a singular verb should be used.

Example: <u>Vincent</u> <u>is</u> a fast runner.

If the subject is plural, a plural verb should be used.

Example: The <u>players</u> <u>are</u> tired.

A. Circle the correct answers.

Fred *1.* play / plays the piano very well.

His parents *2.* is / are very proud of him.

They *3.* don't / doesn't watch TV when

he plays the piano. His piano *4.* is / are

very expensive. It *5.* was / were a present

from his parents. He *6.* don't / doesn't let others play it.

It *7.* was / were my birthday last Friday. Mom

and Dad bought me a dog. He *8.* is / am very

cute. I *9.* call / calls him Kiki. He *10.* has / have

big ears. They *11.* stick / sticks out when I call his

name. I *12.* like / likes playing with him. I think he

13. enjoy / enjoys playing with me too.

      ISBN: 978-1-897457-04-7

B. Check if the underlined words are correct. If not, write the correct ones on the lines.

1. Each of us <u>prepare</u> one item for the barbecue. _____

2. How much <u>are</u> this DVD? _____

3. The <u>thieves</u> was a man. _____

4. Today <u>is</u> Sunday. _____

5. There <u>was</u> a lot of mistakes in his writing. _____

6. Jay <u>or</u> Olivia are best friends. _____

7. Raking leaves <u>are</u> easy. _____

C. In the following sentences, change the singular subjects to plural and the plural subjects to singular. Make changes to the verbs too.

1. The squirrels have eaten our cherries.

   _____

2. The hunting dog is well trained.

   _____

3. The children were swimming in the pool.

   _____

4. This rabbit always hides behind the bushes.

   _____

5. Those potatoes were taken from Grandpa's farm.

   _____

6. These sheep have their wool shorn by the farmer.

   _____

ISBN: 978-1-897457-04-7

Simple Sentences

A **simple sentence** expresses a complete thought. It is made up of a subject and a predicate.

Example: A man is beside a car. (sentence)
A man and a car (not a sentence)

D. Check if each group of words is a sentence.

1. _____ We enjoy sunbathing.

2. _____ The morning sun is soothing.

3. _____ The cool pool water.

4. _____ My lazy poodle.

5. _____ I swim with my cousins.

E. Put the words in order to form sentences.

1. change   leaves   maple   in   fall   colour

    _____

2. it   slippery   snow   is   to   on   the   walk

    _____

3. standing   pole   the   monkey   is   the   on

    _____

4. will   the   puzzle   soon   very   we   complete

    _____

ISBN: 978-1-897457-04-7

Compound Sentences

A **compound sentence** is made up of two simple sentences joined together by a conjunction (and/or/but).

Example: The film was funny. We laughed aloud.
(simple sentences)

The film was funny and we laughed aloud.
(compound sentence)

F. **Form compound sentences by joining the sentences in Column A to those in Column B with suitable conjunctions. Write the compound sentences on the lines.**

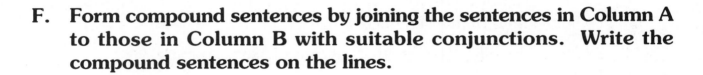

Column A

1. My computer is old.
2. The beach is beautiful.
3. I will join the party.
4. My brother is little.
5. We will watch the football game.

Column B

- I have to leave early.
- He needs to take an afternoon nap.
- We will go out for dinner.
- It is easy to get to.
- It still works.

1. _____

2. _____

3. _____

4. _____

5. _____

ISBN: 978-1-897457-04-7

unit 9 Phrases and Clauses

Phrases and Clauses

A **phrase** is a group of words in a sentence that does not include a subject and a verb.

Example: Let's have dinner <u>at the restaurant over there</u>.

A **clause** is a group of words that has the same structure as a sentence but it is part of a larger sentence. Clauses are linked together by a conjunction to form a sentence.

Example: <u>I joined this program</u> because <u>I like swimming</u>.

A. Write "P" if the underlined parts are phrases and "C" if they are clauses.

1. She can make you disappear <u>with her magic wand</u>. ____

2. <u>To win the game</u>, you need to get all the sticks. ____

3. <u>My hair sticks out</u> when I hear a squeaky voice. ____

4. We turned off the lights <u>at the beginning of the party</u>. ____

5. Even if it rains, <u>Mr. Franco will go jogging all the same</u>. ____

6. <u>He has always wanted to be a firefighter</u> since he was seven. ____

7. <u>Because of the heavy rain last night</u>, the concert was cancelled. ____

8. I tried to call you but <u>the line was busy</u>. ____

ISBN: 978-1-897457-04-7

B. Form phrases with the given words to complete the sentences.

1. The little polar bear always climbs

   _____ .

   (mother's   its   on   back)

2. Gilbert _____
   in the performance. (best   his   did)

3. Mr. Fleet is such _____ that he drove
   us home. (a   person   helpful)

4. Don't call me; I'll be busy _____ .
   (my   homework   doing)

5. The air tickets are expensive _____ .
   (during   season   the   peak)

C. Complete the sentences with the given clauses.

we could finish the project	you go sailing
I'll have orange juice	I came last
it looks like new	
our car broke down	

1. We are late because _____ .

2. I finished the race although _____ .

3. We worked overnight so _____ .

4. Always wear a life jacket when _____ .

5. If you don't have milk, _____ .

6. Dad has polished the car and _____ .

ISBN: 978-1-897457-04-7

Noun Phrases

A **noun phrase** is any phrase that includes a noun and all its modifiers.

Example: We had to drive through <u>a long winding road</u> to get to the campsite.

D. Underline the noun phrases in the sentences.

1. This boring movie made me fall asleep.

2. All of us were impressed by the state-of-the-art cellular phone.

3. They really enjoyed our mouth-watering dishes.

4. The appalling living conditions in this area are driving people away.

5. Mr. Davis has a great sympathy for the blind.

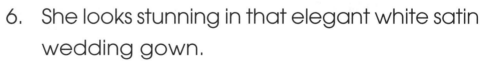

Some sentences may have more than one noun phrase.

6. She looks stunning in that elegant white satin wedding gown.

7. Mom was shocked by this tiny, fluffy creature.

8. Hundreds of people lined up for free turkeys last Friday.

9. The spectacular performance of the circus earned a lot of applause from the audience.

ISBN: 978-1-897457-04-7

Prepositional Phrases

A **prepositional phrase** begins with a preposition and includes a noun or a pronoun.

It can describe a noun as an adjective phrase.

Example: The doll <u>in the smaller box</u> is for Janet.

It can also describe a verb as an adverb phrase.

Example: I decorate the box <u>with paper flowers</u>.

E. Fill in the blanks with the correct prepositional phrases.

> on the first page   of a frog   at the beginning
> with a short tail   at meal time

1. Mrs. Francisco takes care of us _____ .

2. Our cat is the one _____ .

3. Please put down your name _____ .

4. John came first _____ of the race.

5. I want the clock in the shape _____ .

F. Write sentences using phrases with the given prepositions.

1. in _____

2. at _____

3. for _____

4. with _____

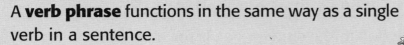

Verb Phrases

A **verb phrase** functions in the same way as a single verb in a sentence.

Example: The wind <u>blows</u> hard. (verb)
             The wind <u>is blowing</u> hard. (verb phrase)

A. **Underline the verb phrases and circle the main verbs of the phrases in the following sentences.**

1. I wish I could ride a real horse.

2. Uncle Ben is working hard to build the fence.

3. They should have tidied up their rooms.

4. We will have a barbecue lunch tomorrow.

5. You should keep an eye on your luggage.

6. They will be flying to Vancouver tomorrow.

B. **Complete the sentences with verb phrases using the given words.**

1. We'd better wait here. It (rain) _____ heavily.

2. They (visit) _____ us next Sunday.

3. The robbers (run) _____ away when I saw them.

4. We (visit) _____ Italy before.

5. You would have won if you (try) _____ your best.

6. Shh! I (watch) _____ the news.

ISBN: 978-1-897457-04-7

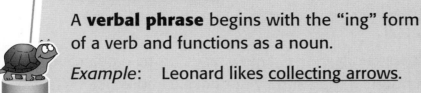

Verbal Phrases

A **verbal phrase** begins with the "ing" form of a verb and functions as a noun.

Example: Leonard likes <u>collecting arrows</u>.

C. Write "B" if the underlined words are verb phrases and "L" for verbal phrases.

1. Gosh! The TV <u>is not working</u>. _____

2. I spend a lot of time <u>working out</u> every day. _____

3. <u>Flying kites</u> is their favourite summer activity. _____

4. <u>Jumping into the pool</u> is what I want to do most. _____

5. The police <u>have been looking</u> into the case for months. _____

6. I'll never forget <u>walking up the stairs</u> to the top of the cathedral. _____

D. Use each of the words to form a verbal phrase in your own sentence.

1. catch

   _____

2. sing

   _____

3. call

   _____

4. write

   _____

ISBN: 978-1-897457-04-7

Adjective Phrases

An **adjective phrase** functions in the same way as a single adjective. It is used to describe a noun. It may or may not have an adjective in itself.

Examples: The man <u>with a beard</u> is Mr. Phil.
He is <u>very kind</u>.

E.   Join the adjective phrases to the nouns they describe.

1. movie   o   o   in its mother's pouch

2. baby koala   o   o   with a hard cover

3. book   o   o   totally outrageous

4. girl   o   o   with a big white bag

5. idea   o   o   near my house

6. restaurant   o   o   terribly scary

F.   Write sentences with your answers in (E).

1. _____

2. _____

3. _____

4. _____

5. _____

_____

6. _____

_____

ISBN: 978-1-897457-04-7

Adverb Phrases

An **adverb phrase** functions in the same way as a single adverb. It is used to describe a verb.

Examples: Mom let the pie sit <u>for half an hour</u>.
Then she put it <u>in the fridge</u>.

G. Fill in the blanks with the correct adverb phrases.

> for our team   in the end   after school
> really hard   high up

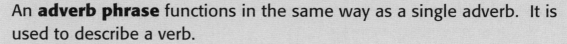

   Yesterday, there was a basketball match

1._____ . It was between our school team

and Island School's team. My classmates and I

made some signs 2._____ . We waved

them 3._____ in the air whenever our team

made a shot. Both teams played 4._____ .

Unfortunately, our team lost three points 5._____ .

H. Write sentences using these adverb phrases.

> near the lake   next Saturday   every summer   to make you happy

1. _____

2. _____

3. _____

4. _____

Quotation Marks

Quotation marks are used in pairs. They can be used to:

- contain the exact words of a speaker or from a book.

  Examples: "No fighting," Miss Dolly said.
  Don't you remember the famous line: "A rose by any other name will smell as sweet"?

- indicate the titles of songs, books, movies, newspapers, etc.

  Example: Do you know the song "A Whole New World"?

A. **In the following sentences, add quotation marks where necessary.**

1. The movie Lord of the Rings won many Oscars.

2. Have you read the book Cat in the Hat?

3. Beauty and the Beast is on at the Princess of Wales Theatre.

4. Mom always watches The Naked Chef for new recipes.

5. Finding Nemo is a popular movie.

6. Jamie asked, Where's the key?

7. We can call it Project X.

B. **Ask two friends what sports they like. Write what they said.**

1. "_____ ," _____ said.

2. _____

ISBN: 978-1-897457-04-7

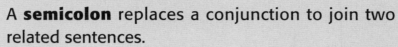

Semicolons

A **semicolon** replaces a conjunction to join two related sentences.

Example: I felt sleepy and I fell asleep quickly.
I felt sleepy; I fell asleep quickly.

C. Match the sentences on the left with the related ones on the right. Write the letters.

1. Tim is a fast runner. _____

2. Dad has a toothache. _____

3. This detective story is very interesting. _____

4. Tomorrow is the last day of school. _____

5. My brother is crazy about SpongeBob. _____

A He has won many medals.

B He has T-shirts with the character on them.

C He doesn't want to eat.

D We need to clear our lockers.

E I've read it many times.

D. Join the sentences in (C) with semicolons.

1. _____

2. _____

3. _____

4. _____

5. _____

ISBN: 978-1-897457-04-7

Apostrophes

Apostrophes are used to show possession or to make contractions.

Possession is shown by using an apostrophe and the letter "s". For plural nouns that already end with "s", just add an apostrophe at the end to show possession.

Examples: This is Benjamin's jacket.
Where is the girls' washroom?

Contractions are single words that are formed by combining and shortening two words. An apostrophe is used to replace letters.

Examples: they are – they're
will not – won't

E. Write "P" for possession and "C" for contraction to indicate why the apostrophe is used in each of the sentences.

1. Strawberry is my uncle's favourite ice cream flavour. _____

2. Who's coming to the restaurant? _____

3. She's read the book before. _____

4. Spencer is Magnus's best friend. _____

F. Fill in the blanks with words using the apostrophe to show possession.

1. This hat belongs to Jordan. This is _____ hat.

2. Those candies belong to James. They are _____ candies.

3. These instruments belong to the musicians. They are the _____ instruments.

G. Complete the crossword puzzle with the contractions of the clue words.

Across

A. who is
B. does not
C. did not
D. there is
E. cannot

Down

1. I am
2. would not
3. they have
4. you are
5. is not

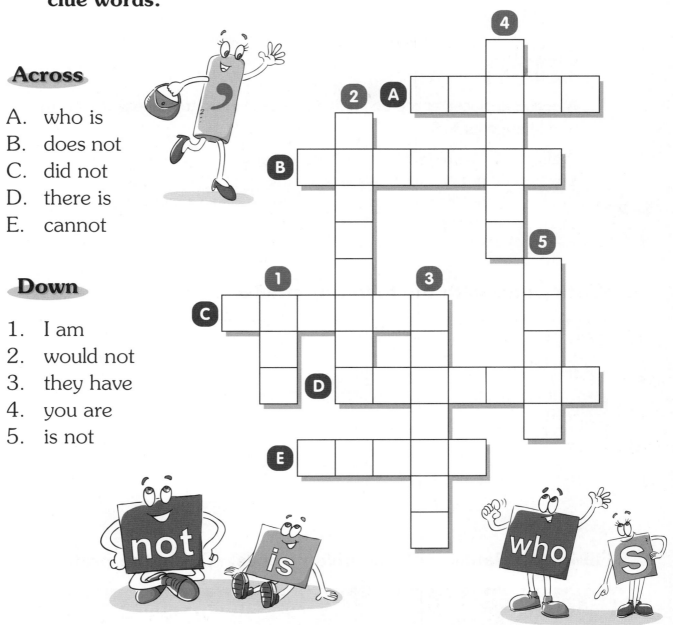

H. Use four of the contractions in (G) to make sentences of your own.

1. _____

2. _____

3. _____

4. _____

ISBN: 978-1-897457-04-7

Prefixes and Suffixes

Prefixes

A **prefix** is placed at the beginning of a base word to make a new word and change its meaning.

Prefix	Meaning	Prefix	Meaning
un	not	dis	opposite
pre	before	re	again
mis	wrong		

A. Write words with the following prefixes.

1.	re			
2.	pre			
3.	dis			
4.	un			
5.	mis			

B. Fill in the blanks with the given words. Circle the prefixes.

mistaken   redial   dishonest   precaution   unbelievable

1. I'd better take an umbrella as a _____ .

2. If you want to call the same number, simply press "_____".

3. I was _____ for my twin brother.

4. It is _____ to keep the extra change.

5. The trick played by the magician was _____ .

ISBN: 978-1-897457-04-7

C. Check the sentences that have prefixes and write the prefixes on the lines.

1. The magician made the rabbit disappear. ◯ _____

2. The cat played with a ball of yarn. ◯ _____

3. These batteries need to be recharged. ◯ _____

4. Many people misspell my name. ◯ _____

5. The hockey game was very exciting. ◯ _____

6. The water runs under the bridge. ◯ _____

D. Write the correct prefix to complete the words in the story.

| un | mis | re | dis | pre |

My mom and I are baking cookies. My brother is at

1. _____school so he is 2. _____able to help us. We 3. _____heat the

oven and gather the ingredients. My brother 4. _____likes nuts,

so we use raisins instead. Even though I know my mom will

5. _____approve, I try to lick the spoon. She says I won't

get to eat any cookies if I 6. _____behave. Just as

we put the cookies in the oven, my

mom says she's 7. _____understood

some of the instructions because

they were 8. _____clear. We will have

to 9. _____make the entire batch!

Suffixes

A **suffix** is placed at the end of a base word to make a new word and change its meaning.

Suffix	Meaning		Suffix	Meaning
ful	full of		less	without
able	able to do		ness	state of being
ly	in a manner of			

E.   Circle the words that use the suffixes above.

My Uncle Jerry is very knowledgeable. He always has some useful information for us. At the beach, he told my sister and me about spineless jellyfish. He said their sting is usually harmless, but it still hurts. He told us we would be all right as long as we paid attention. We swam in the sea cautiously and did not see any jellyfish.

F.   Add suitable suffixes to the root words.

1. Those gloves are very (fashion) _____ .

2. After chewing for a while, the gum becomes (taste) _____ .

3. We are testing your level of (alert) _____ .

4. He (kind) _____ opened the door for me.

5. It was (thought) _____ of Mike to send Mary a birthday card.

ISBN: 978-1-897457-04-7

G. Read the clues. Write the words with suffixes.

In some cases, you may need to change the end of the word before adding the suffix.

Example: in a happy manner – happily

1.	without any use	
2.	state of being weak	
3.	full of hope	
4.	can afford to buy it	
5.	in a hasty manner	
6.	state of being fair	

H. Write sentences using the words you wrote in (G).

1. _____

2. _____

3. _____

4. _____

5. _____

6. _____

ISBN: 978-1-897457-04-7

> **Paragraphs and Topic Sentences**
>
> A **paragraph** is a group of sentences that expresses a common idea. It is made up of a topic sentence and body sentences.
>
> A **topic sentence** introduces the main idea. Usually, it is the first sentence in a paragraph. It tells us what to expect in the rest of the paragraph.

A. For each paragraph, choose the correct topic sentence. Circle the letters.

1. I play basketball with my classmates after school. Although I am not very tall, I am quite good at shooting. I often score the most points on my team. My favourite basketball player is LeBron James. I hope that someday I can play as well as he.

   A. I like playing basketball.

   B. I like LeBron James.

2. Leaves provide shade for people. They absorb carbon dioxide and give out oxygen too. The trunk is a source for making furniture. Trees also provide materials for making paper. Some trees provide us with fruit, such as apples, cherries, and pears.

   A. Trees give us fruit.

   B. Trees are useful to humans.

B. Write a topic sentence for each of the following paragraphs.

1. **Topic sentence:**

    It has a total area of 7725 square kilometres. There are over 1500 lakes within Algonquin Park. It has thousands of species of plants and animals. You can see both deciduous and coniferous trees there.

2. **Topic sentence:**

    Blue whales grow to be about 80 feet long on average, weighing about 109 000 kilograms. The females are larger than males. The largest of the blue whales has a heart that weighs about 450 kilograms.

3. **Topic sentence:**

    We use the cellular phone to talk to our family and friends. We can save their numbers on the phone instead of in a telephone book. We can also play games on it while we are on the go.

Body Sentences

Body sentences explain the main idea stated in the topic sentence. They also add details to it. The sentences should be arranged in a logical order. Often, they will appear in the order that events happen.

C. **In each group of sentences below, write numbers to show how the sentences should be arranged to make a coherent paragraph. Use "1" for the topic sentence.**

1. _____ Cup noodles are easy to cook.

   _____ The name "cup noodles" speaks for itself.

   _____ All you need to do is to pour boiling water into the cup and the noodles are ready to serve in a few minutes.

2. _____ I asked my brother to teach me how to skate.

   _____ After many stumbles and falls, I can finally skate.

   _____ I received a pair of roller skates as my birthday present.

3. _____ She has been collecting bookmarks since she was six.

   _____ My sister likes collecting bookmarks.

   _____ She now has over two hundred bookmarks.

ISBN: 978-1-897457-04-7

D. Write a short paragraph for each topic. The topic sentence has been given to you.

1. Have you wondered why we have to put plastic containers, aluminum cans, and newspapers in the recycle bin?

_____

_____

_____

_____

_____

2. Eating too much junk food is not good for our health.

_____

_____

_____

_____

_____

3. Last Sunday, we went apple picking on a nearby farm.

_____

_____

_____

_____

_____

A. Read the story. Put a vertical line between the subject and the predicate of each underlined clause or sentence.

When they arrive at the garden, Flutter, Buzzer, and Hop are surprised to see that Scotch has eaten all of the vegetables. <u>Hop is very disappointed</u> because he did not get to enjoy any of them. He is also still quite hungry.

"Sorry, Hop," Scotch says, "but there really were only a few leaves left. <u>Otherwise, I would have saved you some</u>." <u>Scotch is lying in the shade, picking his teeth</u>. "Well, I won the race. That was my prize."

"Yes, I suppose you did win but I didn't think that you would eat everything," says Hop. Although Hop wanted some vegetables, <u>he knows there are other things to eat in the forest</u>. As he turns to his friends, ready to head back into the forest, he learns that they have other ideas.

"Hop, <u>that is not the only vegetable garden around</u>," says Buzzer. "In fact, I think I've heard of one that is even better than this one!"

B. Find an example for each one below from the story in (A).

1. a sentence with a compound subject

   _____

   _____

2. a simple sentence

   _____

   _____

3. a compound sentence

   _____

   _____

C. Write the correct form of the verb so that it agrees with the subject.

1. Flutter and Buzzer (help) _____ Hop get to the garden.

2. They (arrive) _____ too late.

3. Scotch (say) _____ he is sorry when he sees Hop.

4. Hop (be) _____ disappointed and hungry.

5. Buzzer (have) _____ heard about another garden.

6. The friends (decide) _____ to try another garden.

ISBN: 978-1-897457-04-7

D. Look at the underlined phrases. Write "N" for noun phrases, "V" for verb phrases, "ADJ" for adjective phrases, "ADV" for adverb phrases, and "P" for prepositional phrases in the parentheses.

Buzzer leads <u>the group of friends</u> (1.   ) down a long, winding path. "I don't think it is <u>very far</u> (2.   )," says Buzzer. "We can cut through these trees to get there <u>more quickly</u> (3.   )."

"Good," says Hop. "I feel tired since I <u>have not eaten</u> (4.   ) today."

The three friends look for more flowers and worms on the way there.

When they find the garden, they see that it is <u>not too far</u> (5.   ) from the first one. Not only is there a lot of lettuce but there are also many other vegetables. Hop delightfully eats <u>a little bit of everything</u> (6.   ), hopping to different areas <u>of the garden</u> (7.   ).

"You seem to have lots of energy now, Hop!" notices Flutter.

<u>To make it a better day</u> (8.   ), Flutter and Buzzer only wish they had found more food themselves.

E. Finish the sentences with the given clauses.

> they are hungry, too   he hopes his friends will join him
> he has not eaten all day   they are very impressed
> the friends look for another garden

1. Hop feels very tired because _____

   _____ .

2. There are no vegetables left in the first garden so _____

   _____ .

3. When they arrive at the garden, _____

   _____ .

4. Flutter and Buzzer are happy for Hop but _____

   _____ .

5. Hop would like to visit this garden again and _____

   _____ .

F. Add in the necessary quotation marks in the sentences below.

1. It is a lovely day, says Flutter.

2. Flutter believes that the song Robin in
   the Rain was about him.

3. Since he likes gardens, Hop would probably
   enjoy the story The Secret Garden.

4. This garden is very big! says Buzzer.
   In fact, I think it is the biggest
   garden I've ever seen.

G. Rewrite the sentences with apostrophes to make contractions or show possession.

1. Hop is not hungry anymore.

   _____

2. Buzzer cannot find more nectar even though he would like to.

   _____

3. These worms belong to Flutter.

   _____

4. The friends of Hop are Flutter and Buzzer.

   _____

5. Scotch does not know that there is a better garden.

   _____

H. Complete each word with the correct prefix or suffix.

1. All three friends are very   help_____ .

2. _____like Scotch, Hop likes to share.   re   dis   un   ful   ly

3. Buzzer starts to lead his friends the wrong way, but he quickly _____directs them.

4. For Hop, time seems to be going

   slow_____ because he is so hungry.

5. Flutter is _____satisfied with the number of worms in the forest.

ISBN: 978-1-897457-04-7

I. Read the passage below. Then write a paragraph using the topic sentence provided.

"Look, Flutter!" says Hop. "There are many worms in this garden for you!"

"Oh, thank you!" says Flutter. The group gathers some worms for Flutter to take back to his family.

"Buzzer, there are also many flowers for you," notices Hop.

"Wow! Look at them!" says Buzzer as he flies over to a smaller flower garden next to the vegetable patch.

"I'm so happy I didn't win the race today," says Hop as the friends relax in the warm sunshine. "Instead I am able to enjoy all these delicious vegetables with my wonderful friends."

There is a fantastic garden outside the forest.

_____

_____

_____

_____

_____

ISBN: 978-1-897457-04-7

Grammar Summary

Subjects and Objects

The **subject** of a verb is the person or thing that performs the action.

The **object** of a verb is the person or thing that receives the action of the verb. There are two types of objects: direct objects and indirect objects.

A **direct object** is the noun or pronoun that receives the action of the verb.

An **indirect object** is the noun or pronoun to whom or to what the verb is directed.

Pronouns

A **pronoun** replaces a noun in a sentence.

A **subject pronoun** (I, you, we, they, he, she, it) is used as the subject of a sentence.

An **object pronoun** (me, you, us, them, him, her, it) is used as the object of a sentence.

A **possessive pronoun** (mine, yours, ours, theirs, his, hers) shows ownership or relationship. It is not followed by a noun.

An **interrogative pronoun** (who, what, which, whose, whom) asks a question.

Verbs

In a sentence, the **verb** must agree with the subject. If the subject is singular, a singular verb should be used. If the subject is plural, a plural verb should be used.

Verbs can be in different tenses.

The **simple present tense** talks about facts, present actions, and habitual actions. Most present tense verbs for third person singular subjects are formed by adding "s" or "es" to the base form.

The **simple past tense** talks about past actions. Most past tense verbs are formed by adding "d" or "ed" to the base form. Others are irregular.

The **simple future tense** talks about future actions. The verb is formed by adding "will" before the base form.

ISBN: 978-1-897457-04-7

Adjectives

A **comparative adjective** compares two nouns; a **superlative adjective** compares three or more nouns. For one-syllable adjectives, the comparative and superlative forms are formed by adding "er" and "est" respectively. For adjectives with two or more syllables, add "more" before the original adjective to form the comparative form, and add "most" to form the superlative form.

Some adjectives have irregular comparative and superlative forms.

Some **nouns** can be used **as adjectives** to describe other nouns.

Adverbs

An **adverb** describes a verb. It explains where, when, how, how much, or how long.

Most adverbs are formed by adding "ly" to an adjective. For adjectives ending in "y", drop the "y" and add "ily" to form the adverbs.

Conjunctions

Conjunctions like "and", "or", "but", "before", and "after" are joining words. They are used to join a word to another word, or a sentence to another sentence.

Examples

- **Mom gives me an apple every day.**

  Mom – singular subject
  gives – singular verb that agrees with the subject
  me – indirect object; object pronoun
  an apple – direct object

- **Yesterday's apple was big, today's apple is bigger, and tomorrow's apple will be the biggest of all.**

  First clause: was – simple past tense; big – original adjective
  Second clause: is – simple present tense; bigger – comparative adjective
  Third clause: will be – simple future tense; biggest – superlative adjective
  and – conjunction that links the clauses to form a sentence

ISBN: 978-1-897457-04-7

Sentences

A **sentence** contains a subject and a predicate.

The **subject** of a sentence tells who or what the sentence is about. A **compound subject** has two or more nouns or pronouns joined by the conjunction "and".

The **predicate** of a sentence is the part that describes the subject. It contains a verb describing the action performed by the subject.

Simple and Compound Sentences

A **simple sentence** expresses a complete thought. It is made up of a subject and a predicate.

A **compound sentence** is made up of two simple sentences joined together by a conjunction (and, or, but).

Phrases and Clauses

A **phrase** is a group of words in a sentence that does not include a subject and a verb.

A **clause** is a group of words that has the same structure as a sentence but it is a part of a larger sentence. Clauses are linked together by a conjunction to form a sentence.

Types of Phrases

A **noun phrase** is any phrase that includes a noun and all its modifiers.

A **prepositional phrase** begins with a preposition and includes a noun or a pronoun. It functions as an adjective or an adverb in a sentence.

A **verb phrase** functions in the same way as a single verb in a sentence.

A **verbal phrase** begins with the "ing" form of a verb and functions as a noun.

An **adjective phrase** functions in the same way as a single adjective. It may or may not have an adjective in itself.

An **adverb phrase** functions in the same way as a single adverb.

ISBN: 978-1-897457-04-7

Punctuation

Quotation marks can be used to contain the exact words of a speaker or from a book, and to indicate the titles of songs, books, movies, newspapers, etc.

A **semicolon** replaces a conjunction to join two related sentences.

An **apostrophe** is used to show possession or to make contractions.

Prefixes and Suffixes

Letters can be added to a base word to make a new word and change its meaning.

A **prefix** is placed at the beginning of a base word; a **suffix** is placed at the end.

Paragraphs

A **paragraph** is a group of sentences that expresses a common idea. It is made up of a topic sentence and body sentences.

A **topic sentence** introduces the main idea. It is usually the first sentence in a paragraph. It tells us what to expect in the rest of the paragraph.

Body sentences explain the main idea and add details to it. They should be arranged in a logical order, often in the order that events happen.

Examples

- **<u>Ada and I</u> <u>are thinking of collecting seashells to make a really pretty necklace</u>.**
(compound subject)   (predicate)

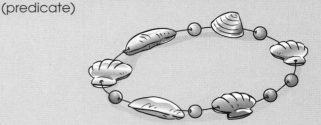

> are thinking – verb phrase
> collecting seashells – verbal phrase
> really pretty – adjective phrase
> a really pretty necklace – noun phrase

- **We'll make it very carefully and give it to Mom on her birthday.**
(two simple sentences joined by "and" to form a compound sentence)

> we'll – contraction of "we will" formed with an apostrophe
> very carefully – adverb phrase
> on her birthday – prepositional phrase that functions as an adverb

ISBN: 978-1-897457-04-7

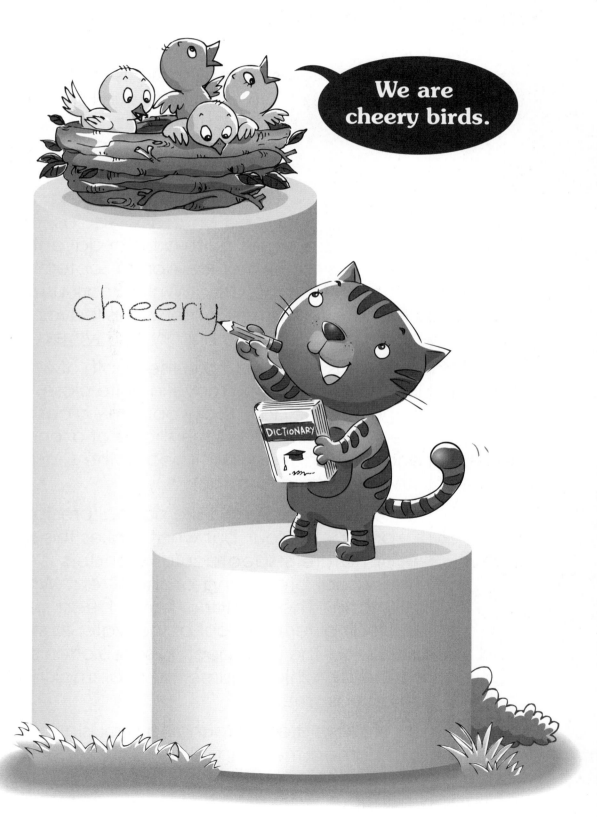

We are cheery birds.

cheery

DICTIONARY

ISBN: 978-1-897457-04-7

1 Seal Island

Seal Island

is a small rocky island about 5 km off shore in False Bay, South Africa. It is home to approximately 64,000 Cape Fur Seals.

At meal times, the seals leave the rocky area to feed on crabs, squids, and schools of fish. This becomes quite a tricky adventure during South Africa's cooler months, April to September. At this time, the fish that the Great White Shark usually <u>forages</u> on migrate to warmer waters. This leaves the seal as the main meal for these hungry <u>carnivores</u>.

Because there is a quick drop in the depth of water from the island, the sharks can move in quite close, yet be <u>camouflaged</u> by the dark, rocky bottom – a perfect <u>ambush</u> zone. The shark follows the shape of a lone or less experienced young seal swimming at the surface, waiting for the ideal time to attack.

This does sound like normal predator-prey behaviour, but what makes this one of nature's spectacular wonders is the unusual <u>breaching</u> of the Great White Shark. These sharks have been seen exploding vertically out of the water to strike and capture a seal. The <u>unsuspecting</u> seal is often sent <u>hurtling</u> into the air, which injures the seal, making it helpless and an easy meal.

This shark stalking area surrounding Seal Island has fittingly been named the "ring of peril" because the Cape Fur Seal risks its life each time it leaves the safety of its rocky hangout.

ISBN: 978-1-897457-04-7

A. Use context clues to find the meaning of the underlined words in the passage. Colour the shark that has the correct meaning.

> When reading an unfamiliar word, look for clues or information in the sentence to help find the meaning of the word.

1. <u>forage</u>   feed   anger   sleep

2. <u>carnivores</u>   animals   meat-eaters   fish

3. <u>camouflaged</u>   tricked   attacked   hidden

4. <u>ambush</u>   trap   home   meal

5. <u>breaching</u>   eating   swimming   leaping

6. <u>unsuspecting</u>   sneaky   surprised   guilty

7. <u>hurtling</u>   catching   throwing   hopping

B. Find 4 words from the passage that start with each letter. Write them in alphabetical order.

s

1. _____

_____

_____

_____

m

2. _____

_____

_____

_____

ISBN: 978-1-897457-04-7

c   p

3. _____   4. _____

_____   _____

_____   _____

_____   _____

Some English words come from other languages and have been changed over time. **Etymology** is information about how and where a word originated.

C. **Combine the Latin words below to create 3 new English words. Using the clues provided, write the meaning for each new word. List 2 animals that would be an example of each.**

"Caro" is a Latin word meaning "flesh".
"Herba" is a Latin word meaning "vegetation".
"Omni" is a Latin word meaning "all".
"Vorare" is a Latin word meaning "to swallow".

1. caro + vorare = _____

    A. omnivore   B. carnivore   C. herbivore

    Meaning: _____

    Examples: _____ and _____

2. herba + vorare = _____

    A. herbivore   B. omnivore   C. carnivore

    Meaning: _____

    Examples: _____ and _____

3. omni + vorare = _____

   A. carnivore   B. herbivore   C. omnivore

   Meaning: _____

   Examples: _____ and _____

D. Imagine that you are a journalist for a wildlife magazine. You have just visited the waters around Seal Island. Write a report with interesting details about your observations.

_____
_____
_____
_____
_____
_____
_____
_____
_____
_____
_____
_____
_____

2 More than Candy

PEZ is a delicious fruity candy that comes with a candy holder that is available in assorted styles of heads. Eduard Haas III invented PEZ in 1927 in Vienna, Austria. It was originally sold in a peppermint flavour. The German word for peppermint is "pfefferminz". Eduard simply abbreviated the German word and came up with the now familiar word "PEZ".

In the beginning, PEZ was a breath mint for adults. The sales, however, were quite low and Haas had to come up with another plan. In 1952, he opened an office in the United States and changed his product and selling strategy. In addition to the mint flavour, he made fruit flavours in different coloured tablets, and he put character heads on the top of the dispensers. The new PEZ was a huge success with children.

Now there are over 275 different PEZ heads, ranging from Mickey Mouse to Santa Claus and Spiderman to Mary Poppins. PEZ is not just a fun treat for children – the dispensers have actually become collector items. There are even PEZ conventions held around the world, as well as a PEZ museum in California.

PEZ's popularity over the years could be due to the everchanging dispenser heads, which keep up with today's characters from cartoons, movies, and comics.

Another possible reason that PEZ has been able to maintain its popularity is the fact that toys and candy have always appealed to children.

ISBN: 978-1-897457-04-7

A. Use the definition, paragraph, and letter space clues to find the matching puzzle words from the passage.

1. interested or attracted (Paragraph 4)

    ___ ___ ___ ___ ___ ___ ___ ___

2. a plan (Paragraph 2)

    ___ ___ ___ ___ ___ ___ ___

3. different kinds (Paragraph 1)

    ___ ___ ___ ___ ___ ___ ___ ___

4. container that holds something (Paragraph 4)

    ___ ___ ___ ___ ___ ___ ___ ___ ___

5. meetings (Paragraph 3)

    ___ ___ ___ ___ ___ ___ ___ ___ ___ ___

6. in the beginning (Paragraph 1)

    ___ ___ ___ ___ ___ ___ ___ ___ ___

B. List 5 different fruit flavours that you would like to see in your favourite candy. For each flavour, write an adjective or descriptive word that starts with the same letter.

	Adjective	Fruit Flavour
1.	_____	_____
2.	_____	_____
3.	_____	_____
4.	_____	_____
5.	_____	_____

C. **PEZ is the abbreviated word for the German word of peppermint – "pfefferminz". Match the words below with their abbreviated forms. Print the letters in the boxes provided.**

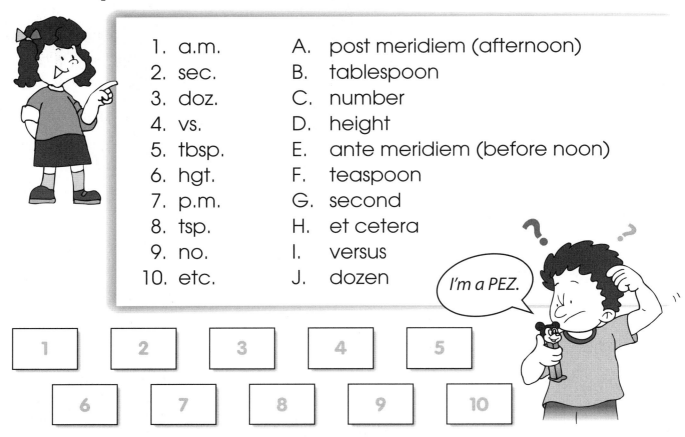

1. a.m.
2. sec.
3. doz.
4. vs.
5. tbsp.
6. hgt.
7. p.m.
8. tsp.
9. no.
10. etc.

A. post meridiem (afternoon)
B. tablespoon
C. number
D. height
E. ante meridiem (before noon)
F. teaspoon
G. second
H. et cetera
I. versus
J. dozen

I'm a PEZ.

1	2	3	4	5

6	7	8	9	10

D. **PEZ dispensers are just one example of the many items that people collect. List 8 other things that are collectibles.**

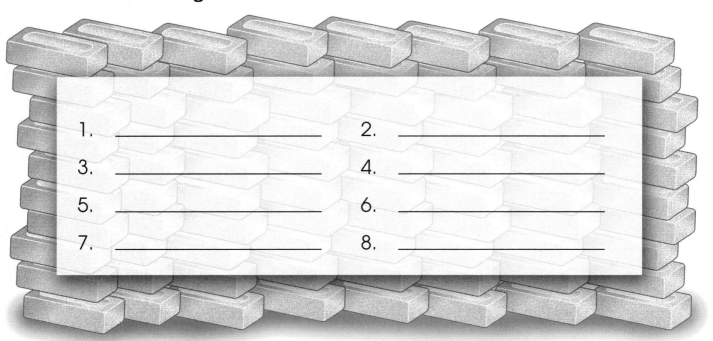

1. _____ 2. _____

3. _____ 4. _____

5. _____ 6. _____

7. _____ 8. _____

ISBN: 978-1-897457-04-7

E. **If you could create a candy of your choice, describe what it would be.**

This may include the product name, ingredients used, how it's made, what it looks like, etc.

_____

_____

_____

F. **Design an advertisement for this new product. Include a catchy title and write three great things about your candy to convince people to buy it.**

Design the packaging for your new candy. Make it colourful and attractive.

3 The Surprise Holiday

David and Kim's parents were very good at organizing activities and gatherings for their family and friends. Early in the year, they started planning a surprise family vacation for their children. Flight tickets were secretly booked, hotel <u>accommodations</u> were pre-arranged, a rental car was waiting at the airport <u>destination</u>, and even the packing was done while the children were asleep!

The much-<u>anticipated</u> day had finally arrived. While David and Kim's father finished hiding the last suitcase in the back of the van, their mother was waking them up for the day. She told them that they would be going on a day's <u>excursion</u>. Perhaps they would go out for breakfast, do some shopping, and spend some time at a park. Kim and David, still feeling somewhat <u>drowsy</u>, did not question their mother about details, and proceeded to get themselves ready. Everyone piled in the van and they were off – but to where?

As they approached the highway exit to the airport, their mother took out the newly purchased video camera, focused it on the children, and began filming. While driving, their father began to reveal where they were headed. It was at this time that the confusion, <u>disbelief</u>, and finally the excitement began. Captured on film were their priceless facial expressions and reactions. Kim and David's dream was going to be a <u>reality</u>. Or was it? Over the shouts, squeals, and laughter, there was the faint sound of a siren. Oops! With all of the <u>commotion</u>, their dad hadn't realized that he was speeding.

ISBN: 978-1-897457-04-7

A. Write the ending of the story.

_____

_____

_____

_____

_____

_____

_____

_____

_____

_____

_____

_____

B. Match the words from the passage with the proper definitions. Write the representing letters only.

1.	accommodations	( )	A.	outing
2.	destination	( )	B.	being actually true
3.	anticipated	( )	C.	places to stay
4.	drowsy	( )	D.	looked forward to
5.	commotion	( )	E.	the end of a journey
6.	disbelief	( )	F.	excitement
7.	reality	( )	G.	feeling that something is not true
8.	excursion	( )	H.	sleepy

C. **Sort the words below under the correct syllable heading.**

drowsy	expressions	everyone	purchased
disbelief	destination	vacation	activities
suitcase	reality	question	reactions

Two Syllables	Three Syllables	Four Syllables
_____	_____	_____
_____	_____	_____
_____	_____	_____
_____	_____	_____

D. **Using a hyphen, show the different ways that these words can be divided at the end of a line.**

Example: **different** dif-ferent differ-ent

> A hyphen may be used to divide a word at a syllable break if you run out of room at the end of a line. The hyphen tells the reader to look on the next line to find the rest of the word.

1.	children	
2.	airplane	
3.	parents	
4.	hotel	
5.	beautiful	
6.	holiday	
7.	directions	
8.	happiness	

E. **Use each word in an interesting sentence. Make each sentence at least 8 words long.**

1. awesome _____

_____

2. silently _____

_____

3. unusual _____

_____

4. enjoyable _____

_____

5. amazement _____

_____

F. **Use the number and alphabet code to find out where David and Kim really were going on their surprise holiday.**

A	B	C	D	E	F	G	H	I	J	K	L	M	N
26	25	24	23	22	21	20	19	18	17	16	15	14	13

O	P	Q	R	S	T	U	V	W	X	Y	Z
12	11	10	9	8	7	6	5	4	3	2	1

15, 26, 7, 4   8, 18, 2, 23, 22, 13   9, 15, 12, 23, 4

G. **Unscramble the coded words in (F).**

_____   _____   _____

4 Hear Ye... Hear Ye! (Part 1)

Edward was a fortunate boy because he was born the son of a nobleman during the Middle Ages. He knew that one day he would become a knight, just like his father. He dreamed of the knighting ceremony where he would be dubbed "Sir Edward".

Finally, the day arrived when Edward could start training to be a knight. He had mixed feelings when he was sent from his home at the age of seven to live at Lord Henry's castle. Leaving home was difficult, but he knew that it was required.

Upon arrival at the castle, the first level of training as a "page" began. Edward learned how to hunt with a falcon and handle weapons and armour. He also spent much of his time mounted on a horse and strengthening his body by wrestling. He knew that these were all skills important for a knight. Edward did not understand, however, why he needed training in manners; he felt that he was already polite enough. In addition to manners, the ladies of the castle also taught Edward how to dance, sing, and play a musical instrument. Edward thought that this was worse than being tortured.

But Edward managed to endure life as a "page" and at the age of fourteen, he graduated to the next level of training as a "squire". Fighting practice was one of his favourite exercises. He was also assigned to be the personal servant for Sir Andrew. Along with caring for this knight's weapons and armour, Edward accompanied Sir Andrew onto the battlefield. On many occasions, Edward had to assist Sir Andrew when he was knocked off his horse or wounded by an opponent's lance. He found these to be frightful experiences. However, with time Edward grew stronger and braver, and he mastered his fighting skills.

ISBN: 978-1-897457-04-7

A. Use the clues below to solve the crossword puzzle. Each word answer can be found in the passage.

Across

A. lucky (para. 1)
B. seated for riding a horse (para. 3)
C. person on the opposite side in a contest (para. 4)
D. struck lightly with a sword in a knighting ceremony (para. 1)

Down

1. went along with someone or something (para. 4)
2. survive or get through a tough experience (para. 4)
3. showed expertise or great ability in a skill (para. 4)
4. long sword-like weapon (para. 4)
5. honourable man of high ranking (para. 1)

B. Each word below has the long "e" sound written as "ea", "ee", or "ie". Fill in the missing vowels on the spaces.

1. pl __ __ se
2. gr __ __ ting
3. t __ __ ch
4. battlef __ __ ld
5. ch __ __ r
6. dr __ __ med
7. qu __ __ n
8. br __ __ f
9. p __ __ ce
10. p __ __ ce
11. f __ __ lings
12. bel __ __ ved
13. l __ __ ving
14. n __ __ ded
15. ach __ __ ve

C. Read the words in each row. Cross out the word that does not belong. Then write what the 3 words have in common.

1. lord   king   friend   knight
_____

2. fighting   teaching   educating   training
_____

3. weapon   servant   armour   shield
_____

4. joust   dance   sing   manners
_____

5. courage   strength   skill   ceremony
_____

D. Write these words under the correct heading. Number the words in each column alphabetically (from 1 to 6).

skills   lady   born   manners
level   castle   training   falcon   wrestling
experiences   lance   riding   lord
ceremony   stronger   knight   fighting   taught

"a" to "h"	"i" to "p"	"q" to "z"

E. Imagine that you are training to be a page or squire. Write a letter to your family describing your experiences and feelings.

Dear _____

_____

_____

_____

_____

_____

_____

_____

At the age of twenty, Edward was deemed worthy of knighthood. He had survived thirteen strict and challenging years of training with Sir Andrew. It was now the eve of becoming a knight. How could he possibly be well rested for the ceremony when there were so many rituals to perform?

As all other squires before him, Edward dressed himself in white. He spent the night in the chapel of the castle, fasting and praying, while keeping watch over his armour and weapons that were displayed on the altar. Edward could scarcely keep his eyes open and his stomach rumbled with hunger. Morning seemed like an eternity away, but then he captured a glimpse of light and realized the sun was beginning to rise. The moment that he awaited for so many years was approaching.

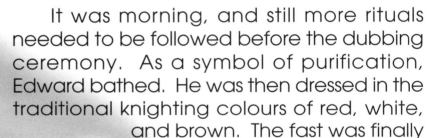

It was morning, and still more rituals needed to be followed before the dubbing ceremony. As a symbol of purification, Edward bathed. He was then dressed in the traditional knighting colours of red, white, and brown. The fast was finally over and Edward was permitted to eat breakfast.

The ceremony was about to begin. Edward was thrilled to see his family and friends present among the crowd. He took his oath of chivalry where he promised to defend the weak, be courteous and loyal, and follow Christianity. He then knelt before Lord Henry and bowed his head. Lord Henry tapped Edward on each shoulder with the flat of his sword and spoke the words that Edward had longed to hear, "I dub thee Sir Edward!"

A great feast followed the ceremony with food, dancing, and merriment. Edward was grateful for the years of instruction he had received, even the dancing lessons.

A. Read each underlined example from the story. On the line provided, print the letter of the matching definition.

1. _____ "the <u>eve</u> of becoming a knight"
2. _____ "so many <u>rituals</u> to perform"
3. _____ "<u>fast</u> was finally over"
4. _____ "an <u>eternity</u> away"
5. _____ "a symbol of <u>purification</u>"
6. _____ "<u>traditional</u> knighting colours"
7. _____ "<u>oath</u> of <u>chivalry</u>"
8. _____ "follow <u>Christianity</u>"
9. _____ "captured a <u>glimpse</u> of light"
10. _____ "<u>deemed</u> worthy of knighthood"

A. based on a belief that is passed on over years

B. a religion

C. cleansing

D. ceremonial behaviours

E. night before

F. judged

G. not being allowed to eat

H. quick look

I. lasting forever

J. promise to show the qualities expected in a knight

B. Write an acrostic poem about a knight.

> The letters of the topic word are used as the beginning letter for each line in the poem. Each line of poetry must be about the writing topic.

Example:

P ractice with weapons

A lways working hard

G raduates to be a squire

E ducated in manners

K _____

N _____

I _____

G _____

H _____

T _____

ISBN: 978-1-897457-04-7

C. Each word below has the long "a" sound written as "ay", "ai", or "a __ e". Fill in the missing vowels on the lines.

1. tod __ __

2. sl __ v __

3. p __ __ n

4. f __ __ th

5. s __ __ ing

6. sh __ m __

7. st __ __ ed

8. pl __ t __

9. pr __ __ se

10. aw __ __

11. tr __ __ ning

12. b __ th __ d

13. aw __ __ ted

14. gr __ t __ ful

15. displ __ __ ed

D. Use the clues to make words that begin with "kn".

Words that begin with "kn" as in "knee" have the "n" sound; the "k" is silent.

1. kn __ __ __ __ → homophone for "night"

2. kn __ __ __ → rhymes with "life"

3. kn __ __ → joint on the leg

4. kn __ __ __ → press and fold dough into a mixture

5. kn __ __ → homophone for "not"

6. kn __ __ → past tense of "know"

7. kn __ __ __ __ __ → rhymes with "buckle"

8. kn __ __ → homophone for "no"

9. kn __ __ __ → past tense of "kneel"

kn __ __ __ __ __ __ __ → learned information

Each page in a dictionary has two words at the top. They are called **guide words**. The guide word on the left is the first entry word on that dictionary page. The one on the right is the last.

E. Circle the words that would be found on the dictionary page with each set of guide words.

decide	**demand**
defend	deem
develop	deliver
deny	determine
defeat	declare

lord	**loyal**
lookout	lovely
loser	lower
longed	loyalty
loud	lost

feast	**festival**
fear	feud
feather	feat
feed	fellow
fetch	feel

tradition	**trait**
tragic	training
trail	track
trap	travel
trade	traipse

F. Each of these sentences has errors. Edit and rewrite the sentences so that they are correct.

1. edward studyed many year too be come a night

   _____

2. wood you like to lived during the midle ages

   _____

3. tomorro edward was dubbed bye lord henry

   _____

6 The Case of the Disappearing Fish

José lived in the suburbs near Rattray Marsh. He had a gorgeous backyard with an <u>abundance</u> of <u>foliage</u>, a variety of flowering plants, and a garden pond with a trickling waterfall. His backyard gave you the feeling of being in paradise.

The pond was José's pride and joy. He had worked <u>diligently</u> to make it a <u>suitable</u> environment for the fish and frogs that he had purchased at the <u>local</u> pet store. It was also the <u>envy</u> of the entire neighbourhood except two neighbours, Jim and Grace.

Grace was an animal lover who believed that animals should not be kept in <u>captivity</u>. She often threatened to capture José's fish and frogs and release them into a natural pond habitat. Jim, on the other hand, loved fish and frogs, especially when they were breaded and deep-fried. He often teased José about sneaking into his backyard to catch a delicious seafood meal.

One Saturday morning, José noticed that one of his fish had disappeared. The next morning, he discovered that another fish was missing. The following day, the same thing occurred. José's fish population was quickly vanishing. Someone or something was stealing them. He drew up a list of possible suspects. At the top of the list was Grace; next was Jim. He also <u>recalled</u> a <u>suspicious</u> cat walking along the fence one day. It could be the <u>culprit</u>.

José decided to stay up one night to capture the thief. He waited outside, hidden behind a bush for hours. It was sunrise and he had almost given up hope, when a large <u>swooping</u> creature came <u>skimming</u> over the top of his head. His eyes widened with disbelief. José had been completely wrong.

ISBN: 978-1-897457-04-7

A. Imagine that you are a detective. Use the following clues to determine what was stealing José's fish.

Clue 1   The thief liked fish.

Clue 2   The creature was large and could fly.

Clue 3   José lived near Rattray Marsh.

Clue 4   The creature's name rhymes with "Karen".

Answer: _____

B. Unscramble the words below and put them together to make a compound word. Each compound word can be found in the passage about José.

Compound words are 2 separate words put together to make 1 word.

1. ase+ofdo   = _____

2. meos+eno   = _____

3. uns+sier   = _____

4. cakb+ryda = _____

5. itsu+leab   = _____

6. esmo+gihnt = _____

7. retwa+lafl = _____

8. uto+dies   = _____

Challenge

hribnoegu+doho = _____

6

Synonyms are words that have the same meaning. (happy – glad)

Antonyms are words that have opposite meanings. (happy – sad)

C. **Complete the word puzzles below with the underlined words from the reading passage.**

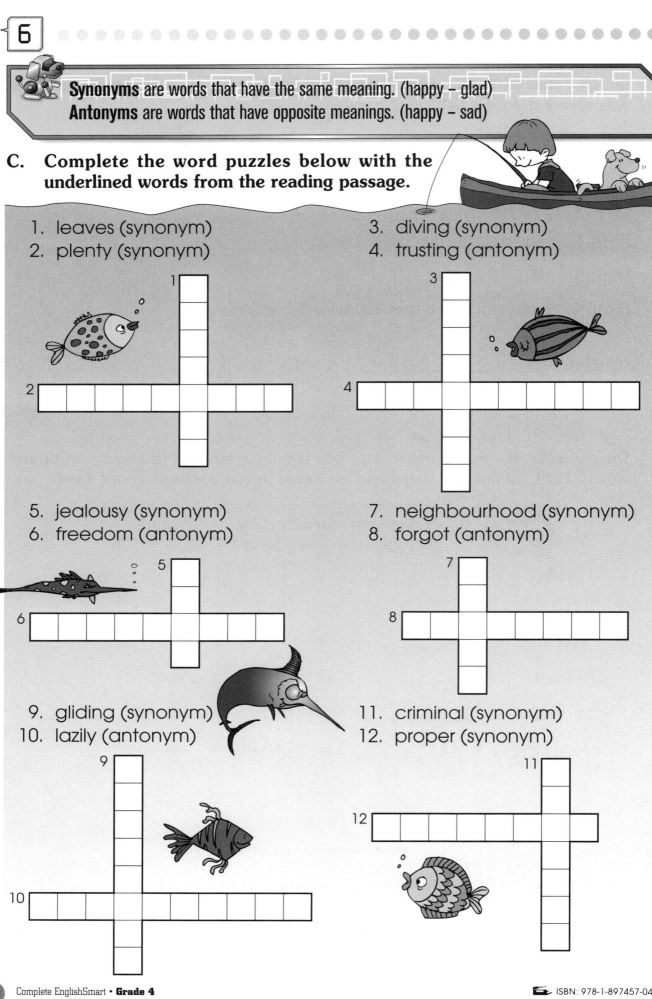

1. leaves (synonym)
2. plenty (synonym)
3. diving (synonym)
4. trusting (antonym)

5. jealousy (synonym)
6. freedom (antonym)
7. neighbourhood (synonym)
8. forgot (antonym)

9. gliding (synonym)
10. lazily (antonym)
11. criminal (synonym)
12. proper (synonym)

184 Complete EnglishSmart • **Grade 4**

ISBN: 978-1-897457-04-7

D. Each sentence <u>tells</u> how José feels. Rewrite each sentence using descriptive language to <u>show</u> in detail how José is feeling.

Example: tell – Grace was angry.

show – Grace's face burned with rage as she stomped to José's house and pounded on the front door.

1. José was proud.

_____

_____

2. José was confused.

_____

_____

The **setting** of a story describes the place where the story occurs. It also tells **when** the story takes place (season, time of day, past, present, or future) and the **mood** of the story.

E. Describe the setting of "The Case of the Disappearing Fish". Illustrate the setting the way you imagine it.

_____

_____

_____

_____

_____

_____

_____

7 Not a Typical Grandma

My grandma is not a <u>typical</u> grandma. I don't call her Grandma because she thinks it makes her sound "over the hill". She prefers Grammy or Grams.

My grandma doesn't look like a typical grandma. Grams has long, beautiful, light-brown hair. When she's swimming or hiking, she puts her hair up in two pigtails, making her look like a Barbie doll. Grams has great fashion sense too. Her <u>wardrobe</u> is exploding with funky outfits. When it comes to <u>attire</u> for an <u>elaborate</u> occasion, she is always "dressed to the nines".

My grandma doesn't live in one place for any length of time like a typical grandma. She has "ants in her pants" because she's always <u>traversing</u> the world. She is presently living in Toronto, where she is writing a book. Last year, Grammy <u>resided</u> in Australia, where she was a student at a university. Before that, she was in South Africa, on safari adventures and climbing sand dunes in the desert.

My grandma doesn't act like a typical grandma. She loves to go rollerblading, whitewater-rafting, and mountain-climbing. Grammy also enjoys tobogganing. She doesn't watch from the top of the hill; rather she is <u>plummeting</u> down the hill at top speed on her toboggan. We go horseback-riding too. She "goes like the wind".

My grandma doesn't like to cook like a typical grandma. When we're together, I get treated to meals at my favourite restaurants and <u>delectable</u> desserts at cafés.

My grandma isn't a typical grandma, but she is a whole lot of other things; she is the "greatest thing since sliced bread".

ISBN: 978-1-897457-04-7

A. Circle the most appropriate meanings for the underlined words in the passage.

1.	elaborate	A. casual	B. busy	C. fancy
2.	traversing	A. phoning	B. travelling	C. reading
3.	plummeting	A. rising	B. bouncing	C. diving
4.	typical	A. usual	B. different	C. same
5.	wardrobe	A. closet	B. bedroom	C. housecoat
6.	attire	A. wheel	B. hairstyle	C. clothing
7.	resided	A. visited	B. lived	C. travelled
8.	delectable	A. delicious	B. fattening	C. expensive

B. Use context clues from the passage to match the expressions from Column A to the meanings in Column B.

Column A

_____ 1. over the hill (para. 1)

_____ 2. dressed to the nines (para. 2)

_____ 3. ants in her pants (para. 3)

_____ 4. goes like the wind (para. 4)

_____ 5. greatest thing since sliced bread (para. 6)

Column B

A. fast

B. old

C. wonderful

D. nicely clothed

E. on the move

ISBN: 978-1-897457-04-7

C. Find four "ou" and two "ow" words from the reading passage. Write them on the lines provided.

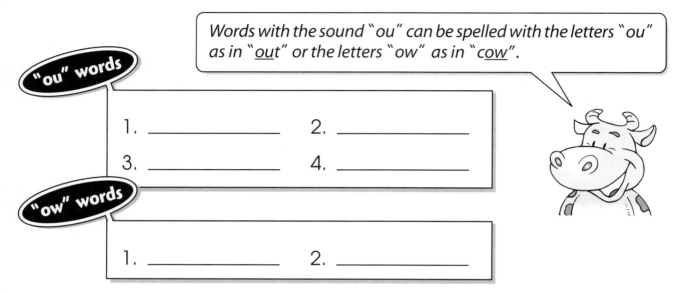

Words with the sound "ou" can be spelled with the letters "ou" as in "<u>ou</u>t" or the letters "ow" as in "c<u>ow</u>".

"ou" words

1. _____   2. _____

3. _____   4. _____

"ow" words

1. _____   2. _____

D. Write the "ou" or "ow" word that answers each clue.

1. opposite of "inside"   __ __ __ __ __ __ __

2. homophone of "flour"   __ __ __ __ __ __

3. worn by a king or queen   __ __ __ __ __

4. opposite of "lost"   __ __ __ __ __

5. used in baking bread   __ __ __ __ __

6. opposite of "whisper"   __ __ __ __ __

7. "Mickey and Minnie..."   __ __ __ __ __

8. opposite of "sunny"   __ __ __ __ __ __

9. "The Fox and the..."   __ __ __ __ __

 **Challenge**

When parents give their children money for helping out with chores, it is called an __ __ __ __ __ __ __ __ __ .

E. Write a fictional or non-fictional paragraph called "Grandma".

> **Fiction** is a made-up story. **Non-fiction** is a true story.

_____

_____

_____

_____

_____

_____

_____

_____

F. List the similarities and differences of the grandma character from the reading passage and the grandma character in the story that you wrote.

Similarities	Differences
_____	_____
_____	_____
_____	_____
_____	_____
_____	_____
_____	_____

A. Read the recipe. Fill in the boxes with the appropriate abbreviations for the underlined words.

> tsp.   avg.   C.   etc.   min.   dz.   vs.
> hgt.   pkg.   lg.   F.   lb.   tbsp.   l.   ml.
> sm.   no.   c.   temp.   med.   pr.

Chocolate Chip Cookies

1. $3\frac{1}{2}$ <u>cups</u> ☐ or $\frac{7}{8}$ <u>litre</u> ☐ flour

2. 1 <u>tablespoon</u> ☐ or 15 <u>millilitres</u> ☐ baking soda

3. 1 <u>teaspoon</u> ☐ or 5 <u>millilitres</u> ☐ salt

4. $\frac{1}{2}$ <u>cup</u> ☐ or 125 <u>millilitres</u> ☐ shortening

5. $\frac{1}{2}$ <u>cup</u> ☐ or 125 <u>millilitres</u> ☐ margarine

6. 1 <u>cup</u> ☐ or 250 <u>millilitres</u> ☐ brown sugar

7. 1 <u>tablespoon</u> ☐ or 15 <u>millilitres</u> ☐ milk

8. 1 egg

9. 1 <u>large</u> ☐ <u>package</u> ☐ chocolate chips

10. Preheat oven to the <u>temperature</u> ☐ of 350° <u>Fahrenheit</u> ☐ or 175° <u>Celsius</u> ☐ . Cream shortening and sugar. Add egg and milk. Add flour, baking soda, and salt . Stir in chocolate chips. Bake for 12 <u>minutes</u> ☐ . Makes or yields 5 <u>dozen</u> ☐ <u>large</u> ☐ or 10 <u>dozen</u> ☐ <u>medium</u> ☐ cookies. Enjoy!

B. **Sort the words below under the correct syllable heading.**

delicious	measure	temperature	mixture
appetizer	preheat	tablespoon	margarine
ingredient	appetite	flavour	decoration

Two Syllables	Three Syllables	Four Syllables
_____	_____	_____
_____	_____	_____
_____	_____	_____
_____	_____	_____

C. **Read the numbered words below. Find the synonym for each in the word box.**

neighbourhood	delicious	clothing
meat-eater	different	judge	feed
forever	meetings	diving
plenty	interested	cleanse
lived	jealous	mastery

1. carnivore _____
2. envious _____
3. appealed _____
4. local _____
5. conventions _____
6. deem _____
7. expertise _____
8. attire _____
9. delectable _____
10. resided _____
11. purify _____
12. eternally _____
13. abundance _____
14. forage _____
15. swooping _____
16. assorted _____

D. Write these words under the correct heading. Number the words in each column alphabetically (from 1 to 6).

grill	recipe	muffins	apron	nuts
tasty	utensil	eggs	kitchen	sprinkles
pastry	serving	dessert	icing	cupcake
	chef	oven	snack	

"a" to "h"	"i" to "p"	"q" to "z"
_____	_____	_____
_____	_____	_____
_____	_____	_____
_____	_____	_____
_____	_____	_____
_____	_____	_____

E. Using a hyphen, show the different ways that these words can be divided at the end of a line.

1. donuts _____

2. raisins _____

3. caramel _____

4. cinnamon _____ _____

5. chocolate _____

6. decorate _____ _____

7. temperature _____ _____

_____

ISBN: 978-1-897457-04-7

F. Draw lines to match the words in Column A with the words in Column B to make compound words. Then write the compound words.

	Column A			Column B	Compound Words
1.	dish	○	○	melon	dishwasher
2.	blue	○	○	scotch	
3.	clean	○	○	holder	
4.	water	○	○	spoon	
5.	butter	○	○	fruit	
6.	tea	○	○	berry	
7.	pot	○	○	washer	
8.	grape	○	○	up	

G. Circle the words that would be found on the dictionary page with each set of guide words.

bagel	banana
baker	ball
baste	balance
batter	basket
bacteria	barbecue

chef	chop
chill	chunky
chestnut	chip
cherry	chocolate
cheese	charcoal

flaky	flour
flatten	flavour
fluid	flipper
fluff	flatware
fresh	flapjack

special	spray
spoon	spread
spice	split
sprinkle	spatula
sponge	spend

H. Read each sentence. Write "T" if it is a "telling sentence" or "S" if it is a "showing sentence".

1. _____ I forgot to put the timer on the oven and the cookies burned.

2. _____ The kitchen was bursting with the sweet aroma of freshly baked blueberry muffins.

3. _____ We had to wait for the cookies to cool down before we could eat them.

4. _____ Every Saturday morning, I help my mother mix the ingredients for homemade bread.

5. _____ The sweetness of the melting chocolate chips made my teeth ache and my mouth water.

6. _____ The smell and sound of sizzling bacon made my stomach rumble loudly with hunger.

I. Circle the word that is the antonym for the word in each box on the left.

1. fortunate	A. excited	B. unlucky	C. nervous
2. drowsy	A. tired	B. sad	C. awake
3. peril	A. safety	B. danger	C. beautiful
4. recalled	A. spoke	B. wished	C. forgot
5. diligently	A. happily	B. lazily	C. perfectly
6. suspicious	A. trusting	B. guilty	C. nasty
7. captivity	A. caught	B. freedom	C. prison

ISBN: 978-1-897457-04-7

J. Read the words in each row. Circle the word that does not belong. On the line below, write what the 3 remaining words have in common.

1. knife   plate   spoon   fork

_____

2. sugar   flour   cake   baking soda

_____

3. vanilla   icing   candles   sprinkles

_____

4. pizza   cake   yogurt   cookies

_____

5. oatmeal   chocolate chip   brownies   peanut butter

_____

K. Fill in the missing vowels in each of the words below.

Each word has something to do with preparing food.

long "a" sound	long "e" sound	"ou" sound
spr ___ ___	gr ___ ___ se	fl ___ ___ r
gr ___ ___ n	p ___ ___ ce	paper t ___ ___ el
t ___ st ___	cr ___ ___ m	gr ___ ___ nd
tr ___ ___	y ___ ___ ld	br ___ ___ n
sc ___ l ___	p ___ ___ l	p ___ ___ nd

8 Being the Eldest

February 1, 2004

Dear Kids Advice Magazine:

Hi, my name is Evan and being the eldest child in the family surely has its disadvantages. First of all, I have to share all my toys and games with my younger siblings, William and Julia. Of course, they don't need to return the favour because I'm totally uninterested in their things. Besides that, Julia and William are always hanging around me. It's especially irritating when I have a friend over. We look for a secluded place in the house where they can't disturb us, but within minutes, they've found us and are asking to join in. I just can't seem to get a moment's peace.

At meal times, I have to eat whatever is on my <u>plate</u> regardless of the portion size or taste. William and Julia only need to try one bite when it's not their favourite food. Not only this, but I'm expected to be cooperative at all times because I'm the oldest and need to be a role model for them.

It doesn't seem <u>fair</u> either that I have more chores to do around the house than Julia and William put together. Plus, when it comes to practising our musical <u>instruments</u>, I have to practise more than double the time. Oh, and the worst part of it all is the huge quantities of homework I get compared to them.

I'm feeling rather annoyed with my sibling situation. Can you please write back with some advice?

Yours truly,

Evan Smith

ISBN: 978-1-897457-04-7

A. Imagine that you are a writer for "Kids Advice Magazine". Write a "friendly letter" back to Evan that will make him feel better. Try to sound understanding and list at least 3 advantages of being the eldest child in the family.

A ***friendly letter*** has 5 parts: date, greeting, body, closing, and signature.

_____
Date

_____
Greeting

Body _____

_____

_____

_____

_____

_____

_____

_____

_____

_____
Closing

_____
Signature

B. Find the matching puzzle words from Evan's letter.

1. a quiet place away from people (paragraph 1)

   ___ ___ ___ ___ ___ ___ ___ ___

2. the amount of something (paragraph 3)

   ___ ___ ___ ___ ___ ___ ___ ___ ___

3. brothers or sisters (paragraph 1)

   ___ ___ ___ ___ ___ ___ ___ ___

4. someone worthy of following his/her actions (paragraph 2)

   ___ ___ ___ ___   ___ ___ ___ ___ ___

Entry words are words listed in a dictionary. They are in alphabetical order and are typed in **bold**. Most words have more than one meaning.

C. Read the entry words below. Choose the correct meaning for each underlined word in Evan's letter. Write the number.

plate (plāt), n. 1. thin flat piece of metal. *The nameplate was on the trophy.* 2. home base in baseball. *The runner crossed home plate.* 3. food and service for one person. *The restaurant charged $10 a plate.* 4. shallow, circular dish that food is served on. *There were four plates on the table.* 5. firm substance that artificial teeth are attached to. *The denture plate was custom-fit to the mouth.*

1

instrument (in′strə mənt), n. 1. tool or utensil. *The instrument used in cutting is a knife.* 2. person used by another for a plan. *He was an instrument in the bank robbery.* 3. measuring device. *The speedometer is an instrument used in vehicles.* 4. legal document. *All members signed the instrument.* 5. device used to produce musical sounds. *My favourite instrument is the violin.*

2

ISBN: 978-1-897457-04-7

fair (fâr), adj. 1. light in colour. *She has fair skin.* 2. following the rules. *It was a fair contest.* 3. not playing favouritism. *The teacher is fair with all students.* 4. not cloudy. *We had fair weather today.* 5. not excellent and not poor. *He is in fair health.*

3

D. The following are some words from Evan's letter. Write the base word beside each.

A **base word** is the word from which other words can be built by adding a prefix (beginning) and/or suffix (ending).

Example: "Believe" is the base word for "unbelievable".

1. disadvantages _____
2. younger _____
3. uninterested _____
4. totally _____
5. irritating _____
6. regardless _____
7. practising _____
8. quantities _____

E. The paragraph below is written in the present tense. Rewrite the paragraph so that it is in the past tense.

Evan loves to climb in the attic where he has a secret hideaway. He keeps his favourite toys and books up there. Evan is also storing Christmas presents for his family in the attic. He makes sure nobody follows him when he escapes to his hideout.

_____

_____

_____

_____

_____

9 The Mud Puppy and Friends

The "Mud Puppy" is actually one of the 19 species of salamanders in Canada. The Mud Puppy, which is <u>distinct</u> because of the three pairs of red gills on each side of its head, lives its <u>entire</u> life in the water. Other species of salamanders spend only part of their time in the water.

A salamander is an amphibian whose long body is roundish in the centre and includes four limbs and a tail. Its eyes are round with eyelids, but it has neither eardrums nor claws. The majority of the 356 species of salamanders in the world lives in warm climates.

Although most salamanders have common features, there are distinct differences from one species to another. The red salamander, for example, has no lungs and breathes through its skin, which must always be <u>moist</u>. This means that its <u>habitat</u> must be on riverbanks or in wet forests. These forest dwellers lay eggs from which <u>miniature</u> salamanders <u>emerge</u>, without passing through the larval stage.

In spring, most salamanders migrate to ponds where they reproduce. The eggs are deposited in the water in little <u>bundles</u> or larger oval masses. The larvae, like the adults, feed on other animals. The metamorphosis of the salamander is usually completed by the end of summer. This is very much unlike its cousin, the frog, whose <u>transformation</u> from egg to adult is very gradual.

ISBN: 978-1-897457-04-7

A. Use context clues to match the underlined words from the passage with the proper definitions. Write the corresponding letters.

1. distinct   _____

2. entire   _____

3. moist   _____

4. habitat   _____

5. miniature   _____

6. emerge   _____

7. bundles   _____

8. transformation   _____

A. groups
B. natural home
C. change
D. unlike others
E. wet
F. come out
G. very small
H. whole

B. Find information about the frog from the library or the Internet. Write how its transformation from egg to adult is different from that of the salamander.

_____

_____

_____

_____

_____

_____

_____

_____

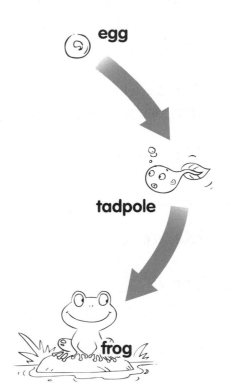

egg

tadpole

frog

9

Prefix Chart

A **prefix** is a syllable at the beginning of a base word that makes a new word and meaning.

Prefix	Meaning	Prefix	Meaning
tri	three	mid	middle
bi	two	dis	opposite
un	not	pre	before
re	again	mis	wrong

C. **Complete each sentence with a word from the word bank. Then use the prefix chart as a guide to write its meaning.**

uncertain	prejudged	triathlete
misread	dismounted	

1. The _____ competed in the swim, bike, and run events.

   Meaning : _____

2. The athlete _____ the rules and was disqualified from the race for going out of the pylon area too soon.

   Meaning : _____

3. It was _____ who would win the gold medal until the final lap of the course.

   Meaning : _____

4. He _____ his bicycle and took some pictures.

   Meaning : _____

5. They _____ the distance between the two towns and ran out of gas in the middle of nowhere.

   Meaning : _____

ISBN: 978-1-897457-04-7

Simile

A **simile** compares two different things, using the word "like" or "as". Use of similes can make writing clearer and more interesting for the reader.

Example: I dive and swim in the water **like a playful dolphin**.

D. **Read the sentences and look for similes. On the lines below, write the two things that are being compared.**

1. The race car zoomed past like a bolt of lightning.

   _____ is compared to _____ .

2. Riding all day in the sun, the cyclist was as hot as sizzling bacon.

   _____ is compared to _____ .

3. His mouth was dry like the desert sand.

   _____ is compared to _____ .

E. **Finish these sentences using descriptive and expressive similes.**

1. Pedalling up the steep mountain, his legs felt as weak as _____

   _____

2. As he neared the finish line, his heart was pounding like _____

   _____

3. The cheering crowds echoed in his ears like _____

   _____

4. Winning the race, he felt as proud as _____

   _____

A. Read the rebus invitation. Rewrite the invitation below without using rebus.

Rebus uses a combination of letters, symbols, pictures, and words to represent a word or phrase.

Helpful Hints:

Plus (+) sign means add the picture and letter(s) together to make a word.

Example: pop + 🌽 = popcorn

A dark capital letter should be pronounced as it is in the alphabet.

Example: dAZ = daisy

~ Invitation Card ~

D + 👂 St + 🂡 + **E**,

U R inv + 👁 + ted to m + 👁 birthd**A** par + 🫖 on ☀ + d**A**, Jul + 👁 1st. It ⭐ + ts at 2 o' + ⏰ and **N**ds at 5 o' + ⏰. We will m + 🍔 at the 🎡 + er 🐴 F + 💪 on 👸 S + 🌳 + t.

Lunch will be hot 🐕 + s, Fr**N**ch fr + 👁 + s, and ☕ + 🎂 + s.

Please b + 💍 🌞 + screen and 🐝 spr**A**.

Y + 🛶 frh**N**d,

🐚 + **E**

_____

_____

_____

_____

_____

_____

_____

_____

_____

B. **Use pictures and symbols to make each sentence into a rebus sentence.**

1. Would you like to race with your horse?

[ ]

2. Can you wait for me at the top of the mountain?

[ ]

3. The rain finally stopped and the sun began to shine.

[ ]

C. Use each of the 5 senses to describe an item from what you imagine to be the perfect birthday party.

Here are some ideas to write about: party location, decorations, cake, activities or games, people, food and drinks, music, and presents received.

sight	
sound	
smell	
taste	
touch	

D. Using the ideas, write a paragraph that will describe this birthday party in such detail that it "paints a picture" in the reader's mind.

_____

_____

_____

_____

_____

_____

E. Use the chart below to answer each clue for the word search. Print the new word in the box.

A **suffix** is a word part placed at the end of a base word that makes a new word and meaning.

Suffix	Meaning	Suffix	Meaning
ful	full of	less	without
ed	in the past	ing	in the present
able	able to do	ness	state of being
ly	in a manner of	er, or	one who

In some words, you may need to change the end of the word first before adding the suffix.

Example: in a sleepy manner – **sleepily**

1. state of being happy	
2. one who bakes	
3. present tense of dance	
4. without thanks	
5. able to excite	
6. full of wishes	
7. one who decorates	
8. without fear	
9. in a usual manner	
10. able to teach	
11. past tense of climb	
12. full of flavour	

11 A Sporty Gal

Laura is an incredible athlete who would be involved in every extra-curricular activity year round if she could have her way. However, her parents view it differently. As it is, Laura's parents do an amazing juggling act of schedules to drop off and pick up Laura at practice and game locations.

During the fall, Laura runs every day on her lunch hour or after school, training for cross-country meets where she races a distance of over 1 kilometre. Following the cross-country season comes volleyball, where Laura is the "setter", considered the most important position on the court.

Right after Christmas holidays, Laura gets in shape for the basketball season. She plays the position of guard, which means she is awesome at dribbling the ball.

As soon as spring arrives comes the badminton team. Laura plays singles or doubles, where she tries to strategically shoot the "birdie" on the opponent's side where it is unreachable.

Finally, near the end of the school year is the track and field season. Laura has great upper body strength and excels at shot put. She also succeeds in high jump, where she does the "Fosbury Flop" technique.

Laura's all-star soccer team kicks in just before summer begins. She plays a defense position, responsible for protecting her team's end of the field so that the other team doesn't score.

As a result of Laura's jammed packed athletic life, she does not have much free time. This sporty gal doesn't seem to mind though, because she is crazy about sports.

ISBN: 978-1-897457-04-7

Transition words help to tie ideas together. They can:

1. show the sequence of events: first, finally, before, after...
2. describe the order things are located: near, over, between...
3. add information: for instance, besides, for example...
4. compare and contrast things: similarly, although, however...
5. summarize or conclude: as a result, therefore, finally...

A. **Find at least 6 transition words or phrases from the passage.**

1. _____   2. _____

3. _____   4. _____

5. _____   6. _____

B. **Read the steps for how to dive in deep water. Write these steps in a paragraph using as many transition words as possible from the word box.**

The first sentence is done for you. You may use the same transition word more than once.

| first | once | then | finally | last |
| after | second | as soon as | third | next |

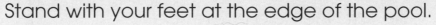

Stand with your feet at the edge of the pool.

Place one knee on the ground.

Stretch your arms over your head together.

Bend forward at the waist.

Tuck your chin.

Push off with your back foot.

Order of entry in the water is hands, head, and feet.

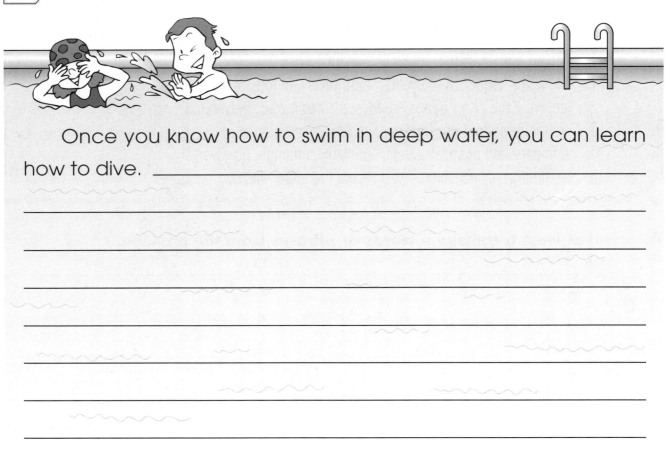

Once you know how to swim in deep water, you can learn how to dive. _____

_____

_____

_____

_____

_____

_____

C.   Read the following sport riddles. Answer each riddle on the line provided.

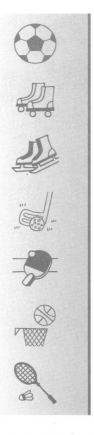

1.   Five players per team on the court
     For this very exciting sport.
     They use a ball that is round,
     And into a net it is bound.
     Two points for that shot.
     A foul it is not.

     What am I?   _____

2.   The first one held in Greece.
     White on the flag symbolizing peace.
     Every four years are the games.
     Athletes from countries of all names.
     Summer and winter it matters not.
     The torch is lit and medals are sought.

     What am I?   _____

ISBN: 978-1-897457-04-7

D. Think of 5 rhyming words for each of the words listed.

Rhyming words do not have to be spelled with the same ending or have the same number of syllables, but they must have the same ending sound.
Example: gl<u>ide</u> – rep<u>lied</u>

score	kick	speed	goal
_____	_____	_____	_____
_____	_____	_____	_____
_____	_____	_____	_____
_____	_____	_____	_____
_____	_____	_____	_____

E. Write a rhyming riddle with 3 rhyming couplets for a sport of your choice. Have a friend try to solve the riddle.

A couplet is a 2-line verse that rhymes.

_____

_____

_____

_____

_____

_____

12 Cornfield Today, Volcano Tomorrow

Imagine standing in the middle of a cornfield listening to a rumbling sound beneath your feet. Then to your fear and astonishment, you see the ground crack open and bulge to about 2 metres high. Smoke and ash begin to spew into the air, followed by a loud, whistling sound. This unbelievable occurrence was actually witnessed by an Indian farmer in 1943, in a Mexican village called San Salvador Paricutín.

The farmer, fearing the worst, fled the scene and returned the following morning to find that this swelling of the earth had grown to a height of 9 metres and was forcefully flinging out rocks. By the end of the same day, it grew another 36 metres. It was the birth of a volcano. Throughout the night, lava shot up over 300 metres and spread rapidly over the farmer's cornfields.

This powerful explosive period continued for a year where the cone of the volcano reached a height of 336 metres. The cone continued to grow at a slower rate for 8 more years, totalling 410 metres. Six months before the volcano died, it had its most violent activity. By the end, over 900 million tonnes of lava had destroyed San Salvador Paricutín and the neighbouring village of San Juan and volcanic ash had choked surrounding forests. Remarkably, nobody was killed by the lava or ash.

Only one building out of the two villages survived this monstrous volcano and did not get swallowed up by the lava. Still today, surrounded by hardened lava, one can see the remains of a church in the village of San Juan.

Although this volcano caused great devastation to the land of the two Mexican villages, geologists had an opportunity to observe and study this volcano from its birth until its death. It was appropriately named Paricutín, after the village where it originated.

ISBN: 978-1-897457-04-7

A. Each word below has the long "o" sound, written as "ow"(gr<u>ow</u>n), "ou" (y<u>ou</u>r), "oa"(m<u>oa</u>n), or "o__e"(sm<u>o</u>k<u>e</u>). Fill in the missing vowels to complete the words.

1. ph __ n __	2. afl __ __ t	3. overfl __ __
4. s __ __ l	5. thr __ __	6. th __ __ gh
7. bulld __ z __	8. cl __ s __	9. gr __ __ n
10. shad __ __	11. rainc __ __ t	12. d __ __ gh

B. Select words from the word box to match with the descriptions. Write the words on the lines provided.

*A word ending in the suffix "**ist**" usually indicates a person who is an expert, or one who works or studies in a certain area. For example, an "art**ist**" is someone who works in the area of art.*

florist
geologist
pharmacist
pianist
scientist
machinist
dentist
violinist

1. one who performs on the piano   _____

2. one who operates machinery   _____

3. one who is an expert in science   _____

4. one who is an expert on rocks   _____

5. one who performs on the violin   _____

6. one who works with flowers   _____

7. one who works in the area of dental health   _____

8. one who prepares medical prescriptions   _____

ISBN: 978-1-897457-04-7

C. **Read the first paragraph of the story. Find 3 words that use onomatopoeia.**

> *Onomatopoeia* is a word that sounds like the thing that it describes.
> *Example:* The bee *buzzed* in my ear.

1. _____   2. _____   3. _____

D. **Draw lines to match each of the following phrases with the onomatopoeia that describes it.**

1. old windows on a windy day   •   • splash

2. eating potato chips   •   • clang

3. eating spaghetti   •   • crunch

4. jumping in a pool   •   • bark

5. washing dishes   •   • slurp

6. sound of a dog   •   • rattle

E. **Write a Word Cinquain Poem about volcanoes. Draw a picture to go with your cinquain.**

> Follow these steps in writing your poem.
> **1st line** – 1 word – title or topic
> **2nd line** – 2 words – describing words about the topic
> **3rd line** – 3 words – actions words about the topic
> **4th line** – 4 words – feelings about the title
> **5th line** – 1 word – synonym for the title

_____

_____

_____

_____

_____

F. Read the two entries and the pronunciation symbols for each set of homographs. Then read each sentence below. Match the sentence with the numbered entry. Write the corresponding letter.

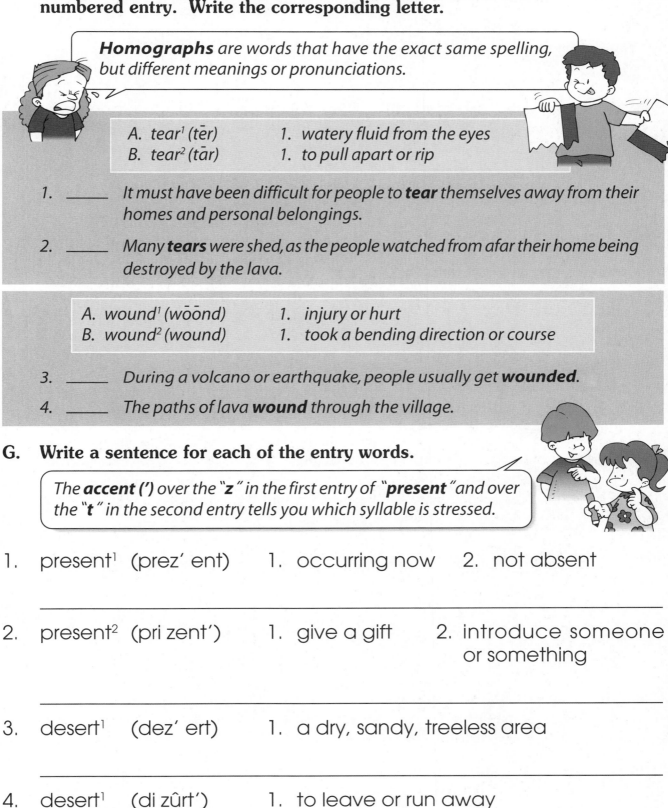

Homographs are words that have the exact same spelling, but different meanings or pronunciations.

> A. tear¹ (tēr)   1. watery fluid from the eyes
> B. tear² (tār)   1. to pull apart or rip

1. _____ It must have been difficult for people to **tear** themselves away from their homes and personal belongings.

2. _____ Many **tears** were shed, as the people watched from afar their home being destroyed by the lava.

> A. wound¹ (wōōnd)   1. injury or hurt
> B. wound² (wound)   1. took a bending direction or course

3. _____ During a volcano or earthquake, people usually get **wounded**.

4. _____ The paths of lava **wound** through the village.

G. Write a sentence for each of the entry words.

> The **accent (')** over the "**z**" in the first entry of "**present**" and over the "**t**" in the second entry tells you which syllable is stressed.

1. present¹ (prez' ent)   1. occurring now   2. not absent

_____

2. present² (pri zent')   1. give a gift   2. introduce someone or something

_____

3. desert¹ (dez' ert)   1. a dry, sandy, treeless area

_____

4. desert¹ (di zûrt')   1. to leave or run away

_____

13 Nature's Fireworks

For thousands of years, the Northern Lights, or in scientific terms, the Aurora borealis, have both amazed and frightened people with the eerie glow that they emit in the sky.

"Aurora borealis" is Latin (the ancient language of the Romans) and means "dawn of the North". The lights are called this because they are seen in the Northern Hemisphere. There is also a version of it in the Southern Hemisphere called the "Aurora australis". These northern and southern auroras usually appear as mirror-like images at the same time in many shapes and vivid colours.

Auroras are caused by particles that are shot out into space by the sun. When these particles reach Earth, they are drawn into the magnetic field that surrounds our planet. When these particles collide with different gases in our atmosphere, the Northern Lights are produced. Since the magnetic field is strongest in the North, that's where you can witness this marvel.

While science gives us the true reason for the Northern Lights, the myths and legends that our ancestors used to explain them are interesting. For instance, the Inuit of Alaska believed that the lights were the spirits of the animals they hunted – the seals, salmon, deer, and beluga whales. The Menominee Indians of Wisconsin regarded the lights as torches used by great, friendly giants in the North to help them spear fish at night. Other aboriginal peoples believed that the lights were the spirits of their people and some an omen of war.

If you ever get to travel to the North, grab some popcorn, settle in a lawn chair, and get ready to watch the best firework show on Earth.

ISBN: 978-1-897457-04-7

A. Use context clues to determine the meaning of each underlined word in the passage. Then look up the word and write the dictionary definition.

1. **eerie**

   My definition: _____

   Dictionary definition: _____

2. **emit**

   My definition: _____

   Dictionary definition: _____

3. **ancient**

   My definition: _____

   Dictionary definition: _____

4. **vivid**

   My definition: _____

   Dictionary definition: _____

5. **particles**

   My definition: _____

   Dictionary definition: _____

6. **marvel**

   My definition: _____

   Dictionary definition: _____

7. **omen**

   My definition: _____

   Dictionary definition: _____

13

Persuasive writing gives an opinion and tries to convince the reader to agree with that opinion by using facts and examples.

B. Imagine that you are a journalist for a tourist magazine. Write a "persuasive" article convincing tourists to travel to the North to see the Northern Lights.

_____

_____

_____

_____

_____

_____

_____

The main idea of a paragraph is usually the first sentence of the paragraph and it is called the **topic sentence**.

C. Write your own topic sentence for the paragraph below.

_____

_____

The Northern Lights can be seen as shades of red, blue, green, yellow, and violet. The most common colours, however, are pale green and pink. They can appear looking like scattered clouds of light or wavy curtains, streamers, arcs, or shooting rays. These colourful forms of light send a beautiful glow throughout the northern night skies.

A paragraph should contain details that fit the topic sentence. These are called **supportive sentences**.

D. Read the topic sentence. Circle the letters of 3 sentences that support the main idea or topic.

> **Researchers have discovered that auroral activity runs on a cycle and is best viewed at certain times.**

A. The "Aurora borealis" peaks or is most visible every 11 years.

B. The last peak period was in 2002.

C. The different colours seen come from air molecules, like oxygen.

D. Winter in the North around midnight seems to elicit the best light displays.

E. Select a topic. Write a topic sentence and 3 supportive sentences that provide details about the main idea.

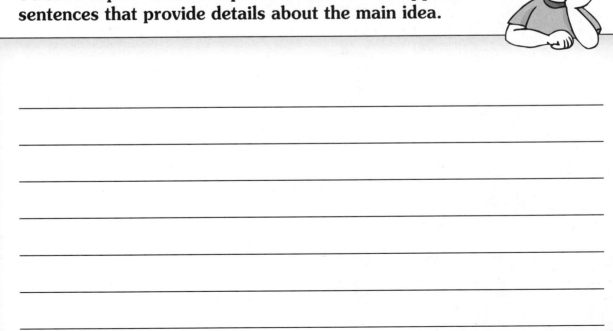

I heard them plead and beg for a pet of their own.
　　A promise of love and care when it was brought home.
Fish, bird, cat, or rabbit would suffice.
But having a puppy would be really nice.

T he pet store was full of pets to adopt.
　　I was the lucky one that day, I thought.
Cuddled in her arms, freed from that store.
Onto new adventures and much, much more.
Romping in the backyard, chewing a bone.
Life was marvellous, I no longer felt alone.

B ut then after months, it seemed nobody cared.
　　The responsibility and commitment was not shared.
The girl got busy with friends and homework, you see.
And I was stuck in a cage again, and wanted to be free.

O ne day I heard the mom argue with her daughter.
　　Constant reminding of my walk, food, and water.
She said I'd have to be sent to another owner.
Someone not so busy; I wouldn't have to be a loner.
My happiness there was coming to an end.
How would my broken heart ever mend?

B ut call it a miracle or fortune, it matters not.
　　It was a wonderful home where I was brought.
The lady was retired and lived on her own.
She longed for a companion; didn't want to be alone.
We were an instant match for one another.
The good times we had – like child and mother.
You'd think I was royalty – always treated like a queen.
Our affection for each other was always seen.

B ut sometimes I think of the girl from long ago.
　　Is she grown, doing well; I'd like to know.
I have no regrets from that time, you see.
She did love me; it just wasn't meant to be.

ISBN: 978-1-897457-04-7

A **stanza** is a group of lines in a poem that has rhythm and a theme. Each stanza is separated from others by a blank space on the page. It is much like a paragraph in a writing passage.

The **tone** is the writer's opinion, attitude, or feeling about the topic. It can be happy, sad, humorous, angry, etc.

A. **What is the writer's tone in each stanza of "A Pet's Tale"? Write the corresponding letter.**

_____ 1st Stanza

_____ 2nd Stanza

_____ 3rd Stanza

_____ 4th Stanza

_____ 5th Stanza

_____ 6th Stanza

A. disappointed

B. serious

C. persuasive

D. happy

E. excited

F. sad

Challenge

Who is telling the poem "A Pet's Tale"? _____

B. **Give an example of each of the following. Using these words, write a paragraph that has a "silly tone".**

A **noun** names a person, place, or thing. (boy, city, dog)
An **adjective** describes something or somebody. (furry)
A **verb** is an action word. (jumped)
An **adverb** tells how something is done. (quickly)

A name _____   A type of animal _____

A place _____   An adjective _____

A verb _____   An adverb _____

_____

_____

_____

_____

_____

_____

_____

_____

Some poets use **alliteration** to make their poems more interesting, humorous, or pleasing to the ear. Alliteration occurs where 2 or more words in a group of words begin with the same letter. They're also known as **tongue twisters**.

C.   Fill in the blanks with words that begin with the same letter of the alphabet.

1.   alphabet letter _____   2.   name   _____

3.   noun   _____   4.   adjective   _____

5.   verb   _____   6.   adverb   _____

Challenge

Using the words above and smaller words if needed, write an alliterative sentence.

Example: Sammy the snake slithered slowly down the slippery slope.

_____

Homophones are words that sound exactly the same, but have different meanings and spellings.
Example: tail – tale

D. Circle the word that matches the picture above it.

1.

sale   sail

2.

dear   deer

3.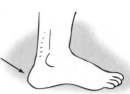

plain   plane

4.

heel   heal

5.

bear   bare

6.

rain   reign

7.

pair   pear

8.

flour   flower

E. Fill in the blanks with the correct homophones.

1. _____ pet was lost somewhere

   over _____ .   (there, their)

2. She _____ her bike down the

   _____ to the farm.   (rode, road)

3. The naughty dog dug one _____

   after another, making our _____

   backyard a mess.   (hole, whole)

4. That _____ does not have grey

   _____ ; it has grey fur.   (hair, hare)

5. I _____ the ball _____

   the window by accident.   (through, threw)

6. When I _____ a letter, I use my

   _____ hand.   (right, write)

15 Camp Wannastay

Friday July 10th

Saying good-bye to Mom, Dad, and Erica was a breeze. I imagined a whole week without my little sister <u>pestering</u> me would be like heaven, but now, I'm feeling differently. It's the end of my first day at camp and I'm <u>dreading</u> the remainder of the week. I thought I was ready for overnight camp, but I suppose I was mistaken.

Saturday July 11th

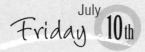

Today, camp went a lot better than I <u>anticipated</u>. Steve, the camp counsellor, is absolutely the coolest. He organized cooperative games so the campers could get acquainted with one another. We also went canoeing and I was paired up with a quiet guy named Shawn. I <u>initiated</u> conversation with him and he became more at ease. Canoeing was a blast. I think we frightened away all the wildlife with the <u>ruckus</u> we created during the splash fight with our paddles. I got totally drenched.

Sunday July 12th

Today was a great bonding experience for the guys in our cabin. The counsellor arranged a competition among the cabins. We came in fourth place in the scavenger hunt, narrowly missing third. The lake water was frigid for the swimming relay, but we placed second regardless. The final event worth the most points was the obstacle course. It was quite challenging, but an awesome time. We put forth our finest effort and it paid off — first place for our team. I can honestly say, the feeling of homesick has completely <u>diminished</u>.

ISBN: 978-1-897457-04-7

A. Match each underlined word in the journal with its meaning. Write the corresponding letter.

1. pestering   _____   A. started
2. dreading   _____   B. noise
3. anticipated   _____   C. annoying or bothering
4. initiated   _____   D. became less or decreased
5. ruckus   _____   E. fearing
6. diminished   _____   F. expected

B. Read each sentence. Find a synonym from the word box for each underlined word. Re-write each sentence.

> extremely   thorough   generous   swiftly   startling   weary
> concerned   scrumptious   brief   lengthy   enjoyable

1. The <u>caring</u> counsellor took a <u>complete</u> look around for poison ivy.

   _____

   _____

2. We heard a <u>scary</u> noise and ran <u>fast</u> to our cabin.

   _____

   _____

3. Although my time at camp was <u>short</u>, I had a <u>fun</u> experience.

   _____

   _____

4. They gave <u>big</u> portions of dessert and it was always <u>good</u>.

   _____

   _____

5. By the end of our <u>long</u> hiking excursion, I felt <u>really</u> <u>tired</u>.

   _____

   _____

C. Write a journal entry for the fourth day at Camp Wannastay. Remember to date the entry and include this camper's thoughts, feelings, and opinions about Camp Wannastay.

_____

_____

_____

_____

_____

_____

_____

D. Write the past tense verbs for the following words. Each word has the letters "gh" in it, which are silent.

> *When the letters "gh" are together, they are usually **silent**, as in "ni**gh**t".*

1. buy _____

2. catch _____

3. fight _____

4. bring _____

5. think _____

6. teach _____

E. Write a word ending with the letters "gh" to match each clue.

> *Sometimes "gh" at the end of a word makes an "f" **sound**, as in "enou**gh**".*

1. antonym of "smooth" _____

2. what you do when something is funny _____

3. when you have an itchy throat _____

4. what a horse drinks from _____

5. meat that is not tender _____

F.   Design a colourful poster to advertise Camp Wannastay the way you imagine it.

1.   Include descriptions of the following:
    a. the cabins and the property around the camp area
    b. activities to participate in – daytime and evening
    c. the people that work there (experience and qualifications)

2.   Include quotations of what other campers say about their experience at Camp Wannastay.

3.   Include illustrations.

Campers' Experiences

A. Complete this story by filling in the blanks with the words provided.

jokes   strong   backyard

company   groovy   best

clubhouse   relationship

Nicole and Madison really enjoy each other's 1._____ . They've been great pals since the time they were born because their mothers are 2._____ of friends.

When Nicole goes to Madison's house, they disappear into Madison's private 3._____ and are gone for hours. The clubhouse is decorated in a 4._____ style and has all the comforts of home. It's equipped with a CD player, books, crafts, board games, comfy chairs, and even a miniature fridge. It's a wonder they ever come out.

After they tire of the clubhouse, you can find them lounging on the giant-size hammock in the 5._____ . Hanging out, telling 6._____ , and sharing secrets seem to be a satisfying pastime for them.

Although Madison and Nicole have changed considerably from the time their 7._____ began, their friendship has never been in question. They've endured difficult times together, but through kindness, trust, and respect, their friendship has remained 8._____ .

B. Underline the base word in each of the following.

1. un<u>success</u>ful
2. <u>fright</u>ful
3. dis<u>appear</u>
4. <u>end</u>less
5. <u>wonder</u>ful
6. <u>perform</u>ance
7. <u>friend</u>liest
8. <u>sudden</u>ly
9. un<u>believe</u>able

C. Build words that match the clues below using each suffix once.

-able   -ist   -er   -ful   -or   -less   -ness   -ly

1. full of wonder   _____
2. one who performs   _____
3. one who writes novels   _____
4. without thought   _____
5. able to laugh   _____
6. in a careful way or manner _____
7. one who sails   _____
8. state of being happy   _____

D. Write homophones for these words.

1. board   _____
2. sent   _____
3. their   _____
4. where   _____
5. been   _____
6. knew   _____
7. through   _____
8. I   _____
9. hours   _____
10. ate   _____

E. Sort these words under the correct sensory heading.

bright   spicy   silky   fruity   blurry   swishing   bitter   squishy
shiny   skunky   fuzzy   crackling   rotten   tangy   whistling

Sight _____   _____   _____

Sound _____   _____   _____

Smell _____   _____   _____

Taste _____   _____   _____

Touch _____   _____   _____

F. Re-write each sentence in the past tense.

1. We practise our dance moves until we master them.

_____

2. Madison and Nicole will attend each other's parties.

_____

3. We study many school subjects together.

_____

G. Find and underline 5 transition words from the paragraph below.

Madison and Nicole keep themselves busy when they're together. First, they disappear into the clubhouse for a game of cards. Then, they check out the fridge for snacks and drinks. After their snack break, Nicole and Madison listen to music. Before they head out to the backyard, they play a board game or two. Finally, they settle in for secrets on the hammock.

H. Find ten pairs of synonyms. List them on the lines below.

> brief bright ruckus wonder swift many start
> oldest fast pester eldest initiate short annoy
> vivid numerous victory win marvel noisy

1. _____ , _____   2. _____ , _____

3. _____ , _____   4. _____ , _____

5. _____ , _____   6. _____ , _____

7. _____ , _____   8. _____ , _____

9. _____ , _____   10. _____ , _____

I. Select a word from the choices below that describe the writer's tone in each sentence. Write it on the line.

> frustrated funny sad frightened
> excited happy angry serious

1. _____ Her body shivered when she heard an unfamiliar sound in the basement.

2. _____ I have been waiting so long for the party day to arrive and it's finally here.

3. _____ Saying good-bye is difficult because we only see each other twice a year.

4. _____ Mom made my favourite cookies to share with my friends at the sleepover.

5. _____ My little sister scribbled all over my homework.

J.   Circle the onomatopoeia word in each sentence.

1.   The chirping birds woke us very early in the morning.

2.   We were frightened at the sudden boom of thunder.

3.   I accidentally dropped the bowl of freshly popped popcorn.

4.   We clanged our glasses together and toasted our friendship.

5.   The mosquitoes buzzed around us while we chatted outdoors.

K.   Choose one of the prefixes to complete the word. Under each sentence, write the meaning of this new word.

| dis | mis | pre | un | bi | tri | re | mid |

1.   The girls had a _____understanding, but they solved it quickly.

Meaning: _____

2.   Sometimes it's better to agree than to _____agree.

Meaning: _____

3.   We were allowed to stay up until _____night.

Meaning: _____

4.   The blue, red, and silver _____coloured room was unusual.

Meaning: _____

5.   The mothers _____arranged a surprise visit for their girls.

Meaning: _____

6.   They were asked to _____lock the door to the clubhouse.

Meaning: _____

ISBN: 978-1-897457-04-7

L. **Match the phrases to create similes. Write the corresponding letters in the boxes.**

1. They ran as fast ⬭ A. as a sleepy bear.

2. Her sweater felt as soft ⬭ B. like a mischievous monkey.

3. Nicole swims ⬭ C. as a tired snail.

4. She was as grumpy ⬭ D. like frosty popsicles.

5. Ben walks as slowly ⬭ E. as a fighter jet.

6. That child climbs trees ⬭ F. as a kitten's fur.

7. My fingers were frozen ⬭ G. like fleeting fish.

M. **Write the letter of the correct answer to each question.**

1. Which word contains a prefix? _____
   A. unity   B. present
   C. disappear   D. middle

2. Which is an example of alliteration? _____
   A. The rattling windows kept us awake.
   B. She is as wise as an old owl.
   C. Nervous Nicole now knows the new neighbour.
   D. Her fingernails are as hard as nails.

3. Which word is an example of a noun? _____

   Which word is an example of a verb? _____

   Which word is an example of an adjective? _____

   Which word is an example of an adverb? _____
   A. groovy   B. happily
   C. clubhouse   D. sing

ISBN: 978-1-897457-04-7

ISBN: 978-1-897457-04-7

1

Write what Mokki the Alien is saying to the children. Use the code to help you.

ISBN: 978-1-897457-04-7

2 Complete the word slides to turn "mice" into "mist". Change only one letter for each slide.

| m | i | c | e |

| m | i | | e |

| m | i | n | |

| m | i | | t |

Complete the word slides to turn "coin" into "burn". Change only one letter for each slide.

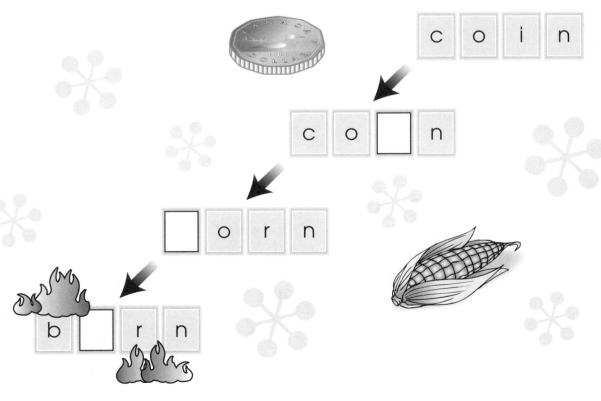

| c | o | i | n |

| c | o | | n |

| | o | r | n |

| b | | r | n |

ISBN: 978-1-897457-04-7

3

Circle the word that does not rhyme in each set.

1.  fish  dish  rich  wish

2.  duck  tuck  luck back

3. star jar for car

4.  lock  look  book  hook

5.  share  bear  pear  dear

ISBN: 978-1-897457-04-7

4 Complete the crossword puzzle with words that rhyme with the clue words.

cross

A. light   B. sleep
C. sigh   D. love
E. hand   F. might

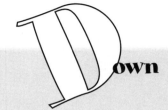own

1. steal   2. tame
3. plain   4. power
5. sale   6. loose
7. bend

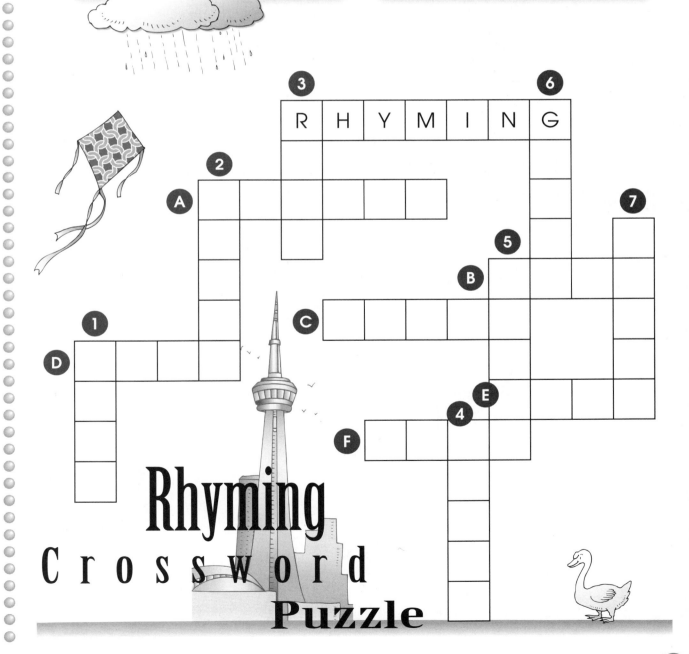

Rhyming Crossword Puzzle

5 Complete the word slides to turn "cone" into "tube". Change only one letter for each slide.

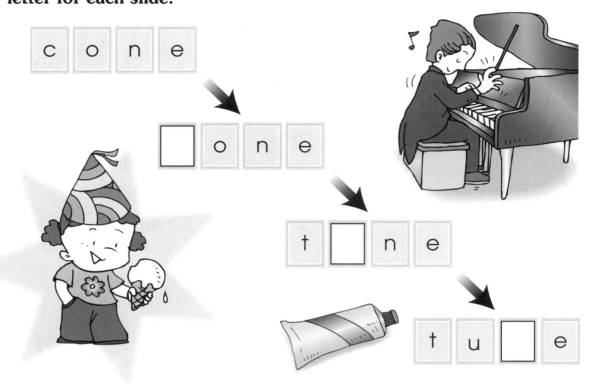

c o n e

⬜ o n e

t ⬜ n e

t u ⬜ e

Complete the word slides to turn "sail" into "tell". Change only one letter for each slide.

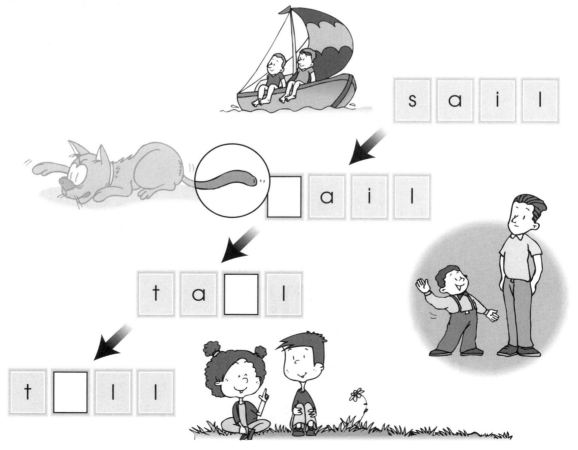

s a i l

⬜ a i l

t a ⬜ l

t ⬜ l l

ISBN: 978-1-897457-04-7

6 Circle the twelve months of a year in the word search.

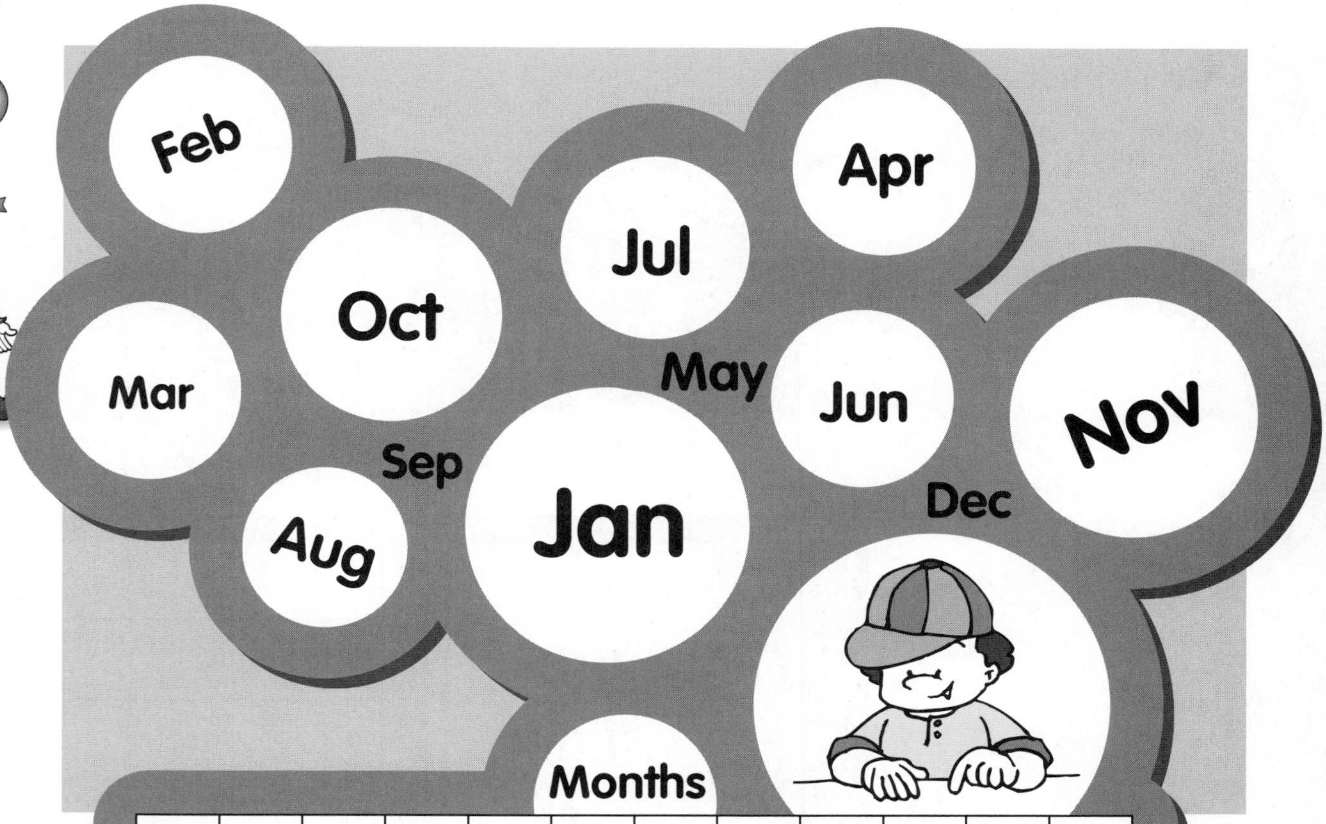

Feb

Oct

Jul

Apr

Mar

May

Jun

Nov

Sep

Aug

Jan

Dec

Months

l	D	j	f	n	D	A	u	g	u	s	t
F	e	O	A	J	h	e	O	l	e	i	d
j	c	b	c	M	a	r	c	h	k	u	N
S	e	J	J	t	N	n	c	S	F	o	h
A	m	g	u	D	o	a	u	M	e	J	k
h	b	M	l	n	v	b	s	a	b	t	a
m	e	o	y	F	e	N	e	y	r	s	y
s	r	e	m	V	m	b	w	r	u	y	n
O	b	J	i	O	b	e	M	g	a	z	k
n	S	e	p	t	e	m	b	e	r	x	p
j	a	k	A	p	r	i	l	c	y	d	r
c	e	o	M	g	D	f	d	i	l	m	e

7 Help Jerry insert the letter blocks into the words in the word machine to form new words.

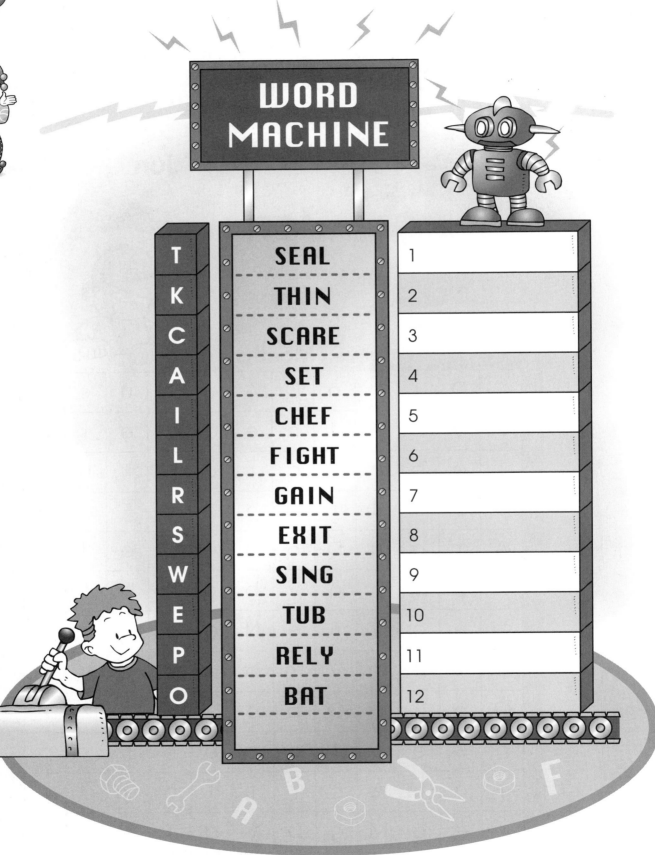

WORD MACHINE

Letter blocks: T K C A I L R S W E P O

Word	#
SEAL	1
THIN	2
SCARE	3
SET	4
CHEF	5
FIGHT	6
GAIN	7
EXIT	8
SING	9
TUB	10
RELY	11
BAT	12

ISBN: 978-1-897457-04-7

8 Complete the word slides to turn "rose" into "dice". Change only one letter for each slide.

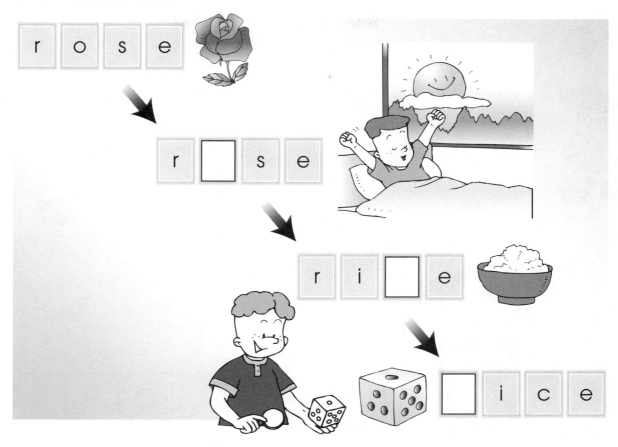

r o s e

r [ ] s e

r i [ ] e

[ ] i c e

Complete the word slides to turn "near" into "bean". Change only one letter for each slide.

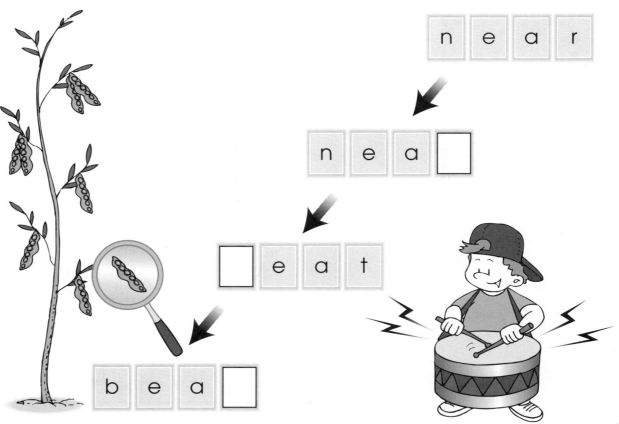

n e a r

n e a [ ]

[ ] e a t

b e a [ ]

ISBN: 978-1-897457-04-7

9

Help Marco the Mouse get to the centre of the maze to meet his friends. Write the plural of each noun.

1. elf
2. ox
3. city
4. deer
5. moose
6. man
7. goose
8. hero
9. child
10. mouse

ISBN: 978-1-897457-04-7

10

Complete the crossword puzzle with a homonym for each clue word.

Across

- A. stair
- B. tear
- C. moose
- D. steel
- E. ice
- F. no

Down

1. caught
2. eight
3. blue
4. right
5. so
6. sell

Homonym

ate = **?**

Help Little Worm get to the core of the apple by following the "fruit" words.

r	u	k	o		c	o	j	i
f	e	t	t	d	e	t	m	a	l	l	b
o	u	a	l	i	m	b	u	v	y	x	p
j	i	v	y	n	a	m	n	o	l	e	r
n	a	o	o	g		e	d	s	m	o
u	n	g	b	v		i	m	r	h	n
l	n	m	a			l	k	c	t
r	f	d	n	w		e	p	e	a	h
w	n	a	e		n	y	s	t
a	a	t	d	u	r	i	r	r	n
b	n	e	c	t	a	k	w	e	f
t	y	e	t	u	e	c	h
j	i	a	p	p	l	d	e

ISBN: 978-1-897457-04-7

12 Complete the word slides to turn "wise" into "wind". Change only one letter for each slide.

w i s e

w i [ ] e

w i [ ] e

w i n [ ]

Complete the word slides to turn "belt" into "wall". Change only one letter for each slide.

b e l t

b e l [ ]

[ ] e l l

w [ ] l l

ISBN: 978-1-897457-04-7

13

Write five 3-letter words with the letters in each group.

1. | P | R | E | A |

2. | B | E | L | E | T |

3. | G | M | T | N | E |

4. | H | R | S | T | I |

ISBN: 978-1-897457-04-7

14 Look at each picture. Circle the correctly-spelled word in each pair.

1.

kangeroo
kangaroo

2.

alien
alein

3.

statue
statute

4.

hammar
hammer

5.

folk
fork

6.

turtle
turtal

7.

toboggan
tobaggan

8.

envelop
envelope

9.

vedio game
video game

ISBN: 978-1-897457-04-7

15 Complete the word slides to turn "road" into "near".
Change only one letter for each slide.

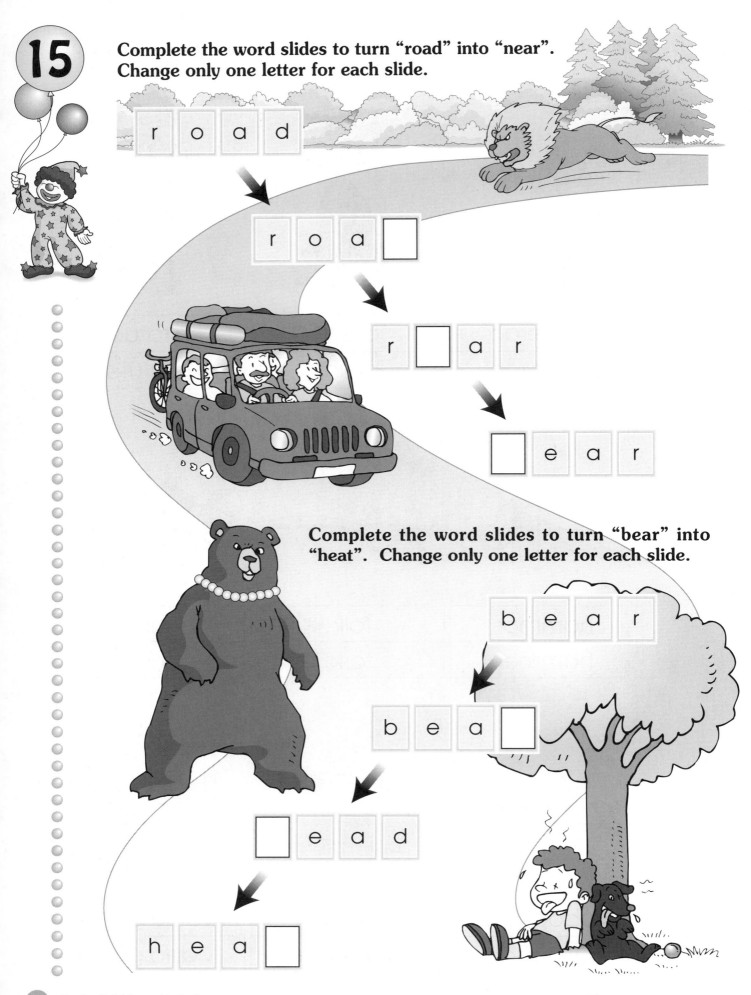

r o a d

r o a ☐

r ☐ a r

☐ e a r

Complete the word slides to turn "bear" into "heat". Change only one letter for each slide.

b e a r

b e a ☐

☐ e a d

h e a ☐

ISBN: 978-1-897457-04-7

16

Circle twelve vegetables in the Vegetable Word Search.

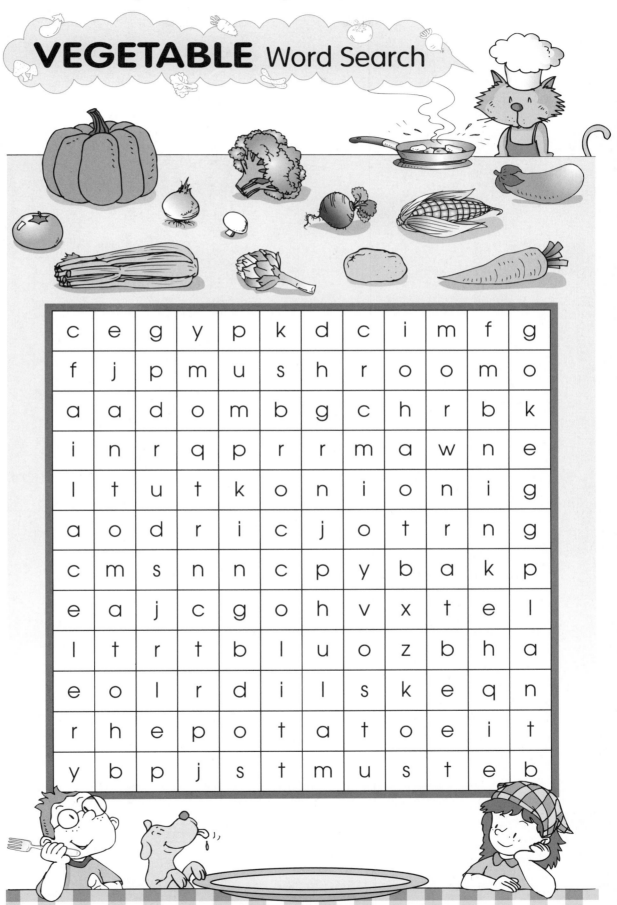

VEGETABLE Word Search

c	e	g	y	p	k	d	c	i	m	f	g
f	j	p	m	u	s	h	r	o	o	m	o
a	a	d	o	m	b	g	c	h	r	b	k
i	n	r	q	p	r	r	m	a	w	n	e
l	t	u	t	k	o	n	i	o	n	i	g
a	o	d	r	i	c	j	o	t	r	n	g
c	m	s	n	n	c	p	y	b	a	k	p
e	a	j	c	g	o	h	v	x	t	e	l
l	t	r	t	b	l	u	o	z	b	h	a
e	o	l	r	d	i	l	s	k	e	q	n
r	h	e	p	o	t	a	t	o	e	i	t
y	b	p	j	s	t	m	u	s	t	e	b

ISBN: 978-1-897457-04-7

1 Animal Adaptation

A. 1. T   2. T   3. F   4. F
   5. T   6. T

B. 1. Adaptation is an evolutionary change that has developed over many generations to help animals and organisms live successfully in their habitats.
  2. They turn white to blend in with the snow.
  3. They need camouflage to cover up themselves when following their prey.
  4. Their natural habitats have been destroyed.

C. 1. cried   2. tired
  3. find   4. hears
  5. behave   6. walked
  7. delicious   8. ran

D. 1. stadium   2. singer
  3. school   4. tower
  5. car

E. 1. E   2. C   3. J   4. G
  5. I   6. H   7. B   8. D
  9. A 10. F

F. (Individual writing)

2 The Human Heart

A. 1. D   2. B
  3. C   4. C
  5. A

B. 1. E   2. A
  3. B   4. C
  5. F   6. D

C. 1. flew ; A   2. played ; A
  3. is ; N   4. were ; N
  5. is ; N   6. sang ; A
  7. was ; N   8. cross ; A

D. 1. went   2. flew
  3. sailed   4. camped
  5. built   6. stayed
  7. took

E.

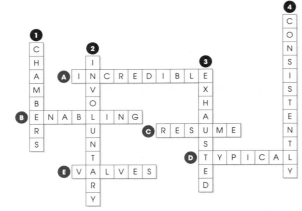

3 The First Heart Transplant

A. 1. O   2. F   3. F   4. O
  5. F   6. F   7. O   8. F
  9. F 10. O 11. O 12. O

B. (Individual answer)

C. 1. excited ; loud
  2. tall ; husky ; heavy
  3. shiny ; new ; red ; perfect ; birthday
  4. tired ; warm
  5. expensive ; top ; antique

D. 1. never
  2. silently ; quickly
  3. gallantly
  4. proudly ; brilliantly
  5. bravely ; courageously

E. 1. its   2. cloths
  3. here   4. dairy
  5. feat   6. fourth
  7. dual   8. weather
  9. dessert 10. loose

F. (Individual writing)

4 The Incredible Butterfly

A. 1. Butterflies have beautiful colours.
  2. They pollinate plants when they feed.
  3. Some use their colour as camouflage while others use their bright colour as a warning. The Magnificent Owl butterfly's large dot on its wing makes predators think that it is a much larger animal.

B. 1. egg   2. larva
  3. pupa   4. adult

C. 1. nectar   2. proboscis
  3. flowers 4. pupa
  5. world   6. Magnificent Owl
  7. Monarch

D. 1. She ; it   2. mine
  3. he   4. they
  5. theirs   6. it
  7. them

E. 1. Which   2. Who
  3. Whose   4. What
  5. Whom

F. 1. exchange ; changeable
  2. imprint ; printing
  3. impolite ; politeness
  4. disbelieve ; believable
  5. impatient ; patience

6. unreal ; realistic
7. indefinite ; definitely
8. misbehave ; behaviour
9. disappoint ; appointment
10. insincere ; sincerity

G. 1. transformation   2. warning
   3. creations   4. widest
   5. diversity   6. tropical
   7. beautiful   8. depending

5   The Atlas

A. 1. G   2. E
   3. D   4. F
   5. H   6. J
   7. I   8. A
   9. C   10. B

B. (Order may vary.)
   1. Atlantic
   2. Pacific
   3. Indian
   4. Arctic
   5. Antarctic

C. Australia ; Asia ; Europe ; Africa ;
   South America ; North America ; Antarctica

D. 1. brother
   2. cabinet
   3. tennis
   4. me
   5. papers
   6. thief
   7. passengers
   8. breakfast
   9. dress ; shoes
   10. flowers

E. (Individual writing)
F. 1. entire   2. globe
   3. circles   4. exact
   5. scale   6. prime
G. (Individual writing)

6   Disasters at Sea (1)

A. 1. B   2. B
   3. B   4. C
B. (Individual answer)
C. 1. dog   2. me
   3. Cathy   4. mechanic
   5. him   6. mother
   7. him

D. (Individual writing)
E. 1. many   2. disasters
   3. left   4. expensive
   5. fancy   6. large
   7. saw   8. fell
F. (Individual writing)

7   Disasters at Sea (2)

A. 1. F   2. T
   3. F   4. F
   5. T   6. F
   7. T   8. F
   9. T   10. F

B. 1. May 30, 1914 ; May 7, 1915 ; November 21,
      1916
   2. passenger ship ; luxury ship ; hospital ship
   3. in the St. Lawrence River ; off the southern coast
      of Ireland ; in the Mediterranean Sea
   4. collided with another ship ; torpedoed ; hit a mine
      or torpedoed
   5. 14 minutes ; 18 minutes ; 55 minutes
   6. 1012 ; 1195 ; 30

C. 1. He | played
   2. parents | told
   3. presents | were
   4. friend | is
   5. two | make
   6. They | played

D. 1. D   2. E
   3. A   4. B
   5. C

E. 1. elegant
   2. spacious
   3. scrumptious / delicious
   4. frequently
   5. drenched
   6. delicious / scrumptious
   7. elated
   8. chilly
   9. depressing
   10. swiftly

F. (Individual writing)

8   Plants – Nature's Medicine

A. 1. G   2. E
   3. F   4. B
   5. C   6. D
   7. H   8. A

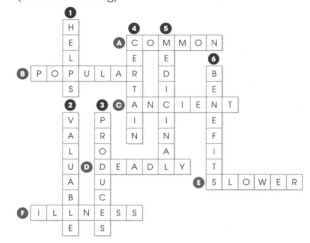

B. 1. T   2. F
   3. F   4. T
   5. T   6. F
   7. T   8. F
   9. T

C. (Individual writing)

D. (Individual writing)

E.

9   Education in the Renaissance

A. (Individual answers)

B. 1. The birthday cake had nine candles on it.
   2. The cat chased the mouse around the room.
   3. The father and his son went fishing in the lake.
   4. School began when the summer holidays ended.

C. (Individual answers)

D. (Individual writing)

E. (Individual writing)

Progress Test 1

A. 1. T   2. F
   3. F   4. T
   5. F   6. F
   7. T   8. F
   9. T   10. T
   11. T   12. F
   13. T   14. F
   15. F   16. T
   17. T

B. 1. C   2. B
   3. A   4. C
   5. B   6. A
   7. C   8. A
   9. C   10. A
   11. B

C. 1. (likes) ; ice cream ; day
   2. (tripped) ; shoelace ; (fell) ; stairs
   3. boys ; girls ; (played) ; yard
   4. Jim ; John ; Sam ; (walked) ; school
   5. Linda ; (is) ; years ; Susan
   6. neighbours ; (held) ; sale ; street
   7. Winter ; (is) ; season
   8. Time ; (is wasted) ; (do) ; nothing
   9. clock ; (struck) ; bell ; (rang)

D. 1. blazing ; slowly
   2. happy ; birthday ; quickly
   3. Slowly ; surely ; skilled
   4. tall ; immediately ; basketball
   5. swiftly ; stone ; sandy

E. 1. her   2. She
   3. me   4. They
   5. she

F. 1. me ; ball
   2. Grandma ; postcard
   3. son ; bicycle
   4. running back ; ball
   5. us ; chance

G. 1. D   2. A
   3. B   4. C
   5. E

H. 1. B   2. I
   3. J   4. A
   5. D   6. C
   7. G   8. E
   9. H   10. F

I. 1. diary   2. fourth
   3. feat   4. whether
   5. duel   6. hear

J. (Suggested answers)
   1. arrangement   2. reorganize
   3. preview   4. disconnect
   5. remind   6. disappoint
   7. dissatisfied   8. creative
   9. disbelief   10. careful
   11. reliable   12. dependable
   13. distance   14. unhappy
   15. priority   16. unknown

K. 1. delicious
   2. hilarious
   3. bitterly
   4. kind
   5. drenched ; pelting
   6. spacious ; antique

10 J.K. Rowling – Her Story

A. B ; B ; C ; B
B. (Individual answer)
C. (Individual writing)
D.
1. un
2. dis
3. un
4. im
5. im
6. dis
7. dis
8. un
9. un
10. in
11. un
12. im
E.
1. kindness
2. terribly
3. careful
4. movement
5. celebration
6. helpful
7. beautiful
8. solution

11 Games and Toys of Pioneer Canada (1)

A. (Individual answers)
B. (Individual writing)
C.
1. sky
2. morning
3. pond
4. school
5. rain
D.
1. moon
2. tuffet
3. hill
4. wall
5. clock
E. (Individual writing)
F. (Individual writing)

12 Games and Toys of Pioneer Canada (2)

A.
1. a stuffed pig's bladder
2. a pigskin
3. hoop rolling
4. a silhouette
5. dolls
6. a tree branch
7. no automobiles
B.
1. O
2. O
3. O
4. F
5. F
C.
1. P
2. C
3. P
4. P
5. C
6. C
7. P
8. C
D. (Individual writing)
E.
1. star
2. canoe
3. pot
4. peach
5. cloud
F.
1. wear
2. hear
3. threw
4. mane
5. weak
6. sail

13 Medieval Castles

A.
1. B
2. B
3. A
4. A
5. C
6. C
B.
1. (In the morning) ; (over the cliffs)
2. of grade four ; (at his desk)
3. in the kennel
4. (under the desk)
5. (up the road) ; (down the hill)
6. (Under the rainbow) ; of gold
C. (Individual writing)
D.
1. knives
2. lives
3. halves
"f" or "fe" to "ves"
4. armies
5. families
6. cities
"y" and add "ies"
7. journeys
8. keys
9. valleys
"s"
E.
1. geese
2. children
3. feet
4. men
5. teeth
6. mice
7. The singular and plural are the same in spelling.

14 The Thinking Organ

A.
1. organ
2. growing
3. process
4. memory
5. emotions
6. cerebrum
7. cerebellum
8. left
9. hypothalamus
10. nervous
B.
1. E
2. D
3. B
4. C
5. F
6. A
C. (Individual answer)
D.
1. and
2. unless
3. since
4. because

5. or   6. while
7. but   8. if
9. so   10. until

E.
1. complex   2. dominant
3. amazing   4. organs
5. mystery   6. emotions
7. connected   8. fear
9. vital   10. creative
11. function   12. stored

F. (Individual writing)

15   The Inca Empire

A.
1. T   2. T
3. T   4. T
5. T   6. T
7. F   8. T
9. F   10. F

B.
1. The Inca were able to build their cities and fortresses on highlands and steep slopes, with stone steps leading up to the top of the cities.
2. (Individual answer)
3. They fought the Inca warriors with guns.

C.
1. ! ; Excl.   2. . ; Imp.
3. . ; Decl.   4. ? ; Int.
5. . ; Imp.

D. (Individual writing)

E.

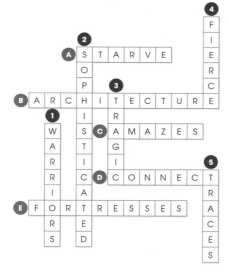

16   The Origins of Money

A. (Suggested answers)
1a. credit card
b. debit card
c. cheque
d. cash

2. It means trading.
3a. shells
b. feathers
c. tools
d. jewelry
4. The item being used for currency directly represented the item being purchased.
5. They could be killed for food or used for work.
6. The shrewdest trader profited the most.

B. (Individual answer)

C.
     In the month of June, Professor Smith took Jake and Jordan on a fishing trip up to Moon River in the Muskoka area of Northern Ontario. The drive from Toronto took three hours but they stopped for lunch at McDonald's. Because the drive was so long, Jordan brought his book entitled The Best Way to Catch Fish. He thought this book might help him learn how to fish. He was going to use the special fish hook that he received for a birthday gift in May. It was made by Acme Fishing Gear Company located in Montreal. When they arrived, they passed the old St. Luke's Church down the road from the river. Working outside the church was Pastor Rodgers, who also likes to fish. He waved at them as they went by.

D. (Individual writing)

17   New France – the Beginning of Canada (1)

A.
1. T   2. T
3. F   4. T
5. T   6. T
7. F   8. T
9. T   10. F
11. T   12. T

B.
1. 1534 ; 1535
2. 2 ships and 60 men ; 3 ships and 110 men
3. Explored P.E.I. and New Brunswick, claimed land for France, brought back Donnaconna's sons, reached Montreal, named village Mount Réal

C.
1. She screamed, "Look out!"
2. The teacher said, "Tonight for homework, you have Math, Science, and Spelling."
3. He played baseball, soccer, basketball, and hockey.
4. "Let's go swimming," said Janet to her friends.
5. Linda yelled, "Is anyone there?"

D. (Individual answer)

 Answers

E. 1.
```
      R
D I S C O V E R
      U
      T
      E
```

2.
```
  I
  M
I M P A S S A B L E
  R
  E
  S
  S
```

3.
```
        F
        O
E X P L O R E D
        T
        H
        O
        L
        D
```

4.
```
            O
            N
E S T A B L I S H E D
            E
            T
```

5.
```
  S
  H
C O N V I N C E D
  R
  T
  A
  G
  E
```

6.
```
  S
  E
  V
R I V A L S
  E
  R
  E
```

18 New France – the Beginning of Canada (2)

A. 1. O   2. O   3. F   4. F
    5. O   6. F   7. O   8. O
    9. O

B. (Individual answers)

C. (Suggested answer)
    He overlooked the furs of the woodland animals such as foxes and beavers.

D. (Individual writing)

E. (Suggested answers)
    1. Carol called on Julie but Julie was not home.
    2. Because Friday is a holiday, there is no school.
    3. My grade four teacher, Mrs. Smith, is nice.
    4. Philip had a doctor's appointment on Tuesday.

F. Puzzle A

Puzzle B
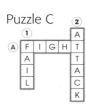

Puzzle C

```
       (2)
   (1)   A
(A) F I G H T
   A     T
   I     A
   L     C
         K
```

Progress Test 2

A. 1. B   2. B   3. A   4. C
    5. C   6. A   7. C   8. C
    9. C   10. A   11. C   12. B
    13. A   14. B   15. A   16. C
    17. A   18. B   19. C   20. C

B. 1. under   2. in
    3. around   4. down

C. 1. P   2. C
    3. C   4. P

D. 1. ADV   2. ADJ
    3. ADJ ; ADV   4. ADV
    5. ADJ

E. 1. but   2. if
    3. or   4. although

F. 1. Mr. Smith asked John to meet him at Lions Stadium.
    2. She said, "Could someone please assist me?"
    3. Lauren and Kara read a Judy Blume story.
    4. Peaches, plums, pears, and nectarines are expensive in winter.
    5. He shouted, "Let me in! It's cold outside."

G. 1. Get up now. ; imperative
    2. Who will help with the work? ; interrogative
    3. Wow! ; exclamatory
    4. This is the main street in town. ; declarative

H. 1. F   2. G   3. J   4. I
    5. B   6. D   7. E   8. A
    9. C   10. H

I. 1. laughed   2. beautiful
    3. chirping   4. dangerous
    5. performing   6. happily
    7. donation   8. reliable
    9. lively   10. terrified

J. 1. insincere   2. indirect
    3. impatient   4. disbelief
    5. unknown   6. improper
    7. misbehave   8. uncertain
    9. unbelievable

K. 1. heroes   2. armies
    3. cities   4. ladies
    5. lives   6. leaves
    7. halves   8. tomatoes
    9. geese   10. mice

1 Subjects and Objects

A. 1. Joe   2. The mouse
    3. The tallest girl   4. They
    5. He   6. Helen's goal
B. (Individual writing)
C. 1. the students   2. your name
    3. music   4. car
    5. mouse
D. 1. me   2. tent
    3. bikes   4. camera
    5. photos   6. sandwiches
    7. fish   8. stars
E. gardening ; many plants ; fruit trees ; flowers ; herbs ; the
    plants ; some flowers ; them ; the room
F. (Individual writing)
G. 1. D   2. I
    3. D   4. I
    5. I   6. D
H. (Individual writing)

2 Pronouns

A. 1. They   2. We
    3. them   4. She
    5. her   6. us
    7. me   8. I
    9. She   10. It
    11. him   12. he
    13. We
B. 1. This present is his.
    2. These cards are yours.
    3. This bed is theirs.
    4. That lunch box is hers.
    5. These photo albums are mine.
    6. This secret is ours.
C. 1. Which   2. whom
    3. What   4. Whose
    5. Who   6. Who
    7. Which
D. 1. Which   2. What
    3. whom   4. ✔
    5. ✔   6. Who
    7. ✔
E. 1. Who put my boot here?
    2. What did he find in the box?
    3. Whose are these?
    4. Which should I take?
    5. Who took this scary picture?
    6. Whom will you take to the concert?
    7. Whose is the highest one?
    8. Which have you chosen?
F. (Individual writing)

3 Verbs

A. likes ; says ; gives ; takes ; tries ; orders ; likes ; says ; hates ;
    is ; is ; go ; watches ; play ; eat
B. 1. drink   2. washes
    3. studies   4. is
    5. feels
C. 1. played   2. decided
    3. noticed   4. asked
    5. said   6. used
    7. lived   8. kept
    9. rang
D. 1. wrote ; gave   2. spoke
    3. whistled ; boiled   4. took
    5. fell ; sat ; waited
E. 1. ✔   2. will make
    3. ✔   4. will help
    5. ✔   6. ✔
    7. will take
F. 1. will see   2. will come
    3. will bake   4. will be
    5. will go
G. 1. Past   2. Future
    3. Present   4. Present
    5. Past   6. Future
    7. Past   8. Present
    9. Future
H. 1. Sam won the gold medal in the long jump.
    2. It will be rainy tomorrow.
    3. The hurricane brought a lot of rain last week.
    4. Every winter, my brother and I make a snowman.
    5. The Parliament Buildings are in Ottawa.

4 Adjectives

A. 1. more comfortable
    2. newer
    3. cheaper
    4. more difficult
    5. easier
    6. brighter
B. 1. more tiring than
    2. more capable than
    3. stronger than
    4. slimmer than
    5. more interesting than
C. 1. smaller ; smallest
    2. worse ; worst
    3. famous ; more famous
    4. happier ; happiest
    5. colourful ; most colourful
    6. lesser ; least

D. 1. the thickest
    2. the oldest
    3. the most wanted
    4. the scariest
    5. the most active

E.
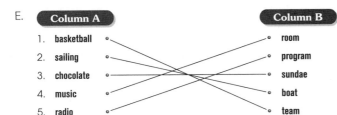

Column A	Column B
1. basketball	room
2. sailing	program
3. chocolate	sundae
4. music	boat
5. radio	team

F. 1. cherry pie   2. treasure box
    3. fish bowl   4. coffee mug
    5. pencil sharpener
G. (Individual writing)
H. 1. toy   2. tennis
    3. video   4. hair
    5. diamond   6. traffic
    7. birthday   8. pizza
    9. alarm   10. cotton

5 Adverbs

A. 1. later   2. carelessly
    3. hard   4. usually
    5. yesterday   6. easily
    7. hardly   8. here
    9. well
B. 1. good ; time   2. good ; show
    3. well ; did   4. good ; me
    5. good ; job   6. well ; play
    7. well ; went
C. (Individual writing)
D. (Underline these words.)
    1. quickly   2. cautiously
    3. specially   4. awfully
    5. seriously   6. patiently
    7. easily   8. solemnly
    9. thoughtfully   10. suddenly
   11. thoroughly   12. swiftly
E. 1. early   2. quietly / patiently
    3. patiently / quietly 4. softly
    5. quickly   6. Unfortunately
    7. Luckily   8. happily
F. 1. surprisingly   2. merrily
    3. terribly   4. anxiously
    5. clearly   6. greedily
G. (Individual writing)

6 Conjunctions

A. 1. and   2. but
    3. or   4. and
    5. and   6. but ; or
    7. or   8. and
    9. and
B. 1. Owls and bats sleep during the day and hunt at night.
    2. The days are hot in the summer but cold in the winter.
    3. We can take the midnight flight or we can take the morning flight the next day.
    4. Greg doesn't like to eat spinach but he likes to eat broccoli.
    5. You can go there to apply in person or fax the form to them.
C. 1. before   2. after
    3. Before   4. after
    5. after   6. before
    7. After   8. After
    9. Before
D. 1. Before you get started
    2. After you melt the butter
    3. After you stir in the Rice Krispies
    4. before you pat down the mixture
    5. before you cut it into squares

Progress Test 1

A. (Circle these subjects.)
    Hop and Scotch ; lots of leaves and grasses ; They ; It ; they
    It ; They ; Scotch ; I ; I
    I ; Hop ; It
    Scotch ; I ; he
    Hop ; he ; they ; Hop and Scotch ; It
B. 1. the garden
    2. Hop and Scotch
    3. Scotch
    4. Hop
    5. Hop and Scotch
    6. Hop
C. 1. vegetables
    2. lettuce
    3. garden
    4. forest
    5. farmer
D. 1. meet
    2. are
    3. am
    4. need
    5. hops
    6. says

ISBN: 978-1-897457-04-7

E. 1. Buzzer is a bumblebee.
   2. Hop helped Buzzer.
   3. Buzzer and Hop will find the flowers.
   4. Scotch will race anyone willing to race him.
F. 1. more competitive
   2. friendlier
   3. faster
   4. smaller
   5. more beautiful
   6. tastier
G. 1. Scotch is the greediest animal in the forest.
   2. Lettuce is the most popular vegetable in the garden.
   3. Of all of the friends in the forest, Buzzer and Hop are the greatest friends.
   4. There are many different ways to get to the garden, but Hop and Scotch want the fastest way.
H. 1. hard
   2. kindly
   3. happily
   4. quickly
   5. fast
   6. suddenly
I. (Individual writing)
J. (Underline these conjunctions.)
   or ; and ; after ; and ; but ; before ; but
K. 1. after
   2. before
   3. but
   4. and

7 Sentences (1)

A. (Underline these subjects.)
   I ; We ; My favourite activity ; Hats, beaded bracelets, and dream catchers ; I ; She
B. (Individual writing)
C. (Individual writing)
D. 1. I | finished my homework.
   2. (Jill and I) | are going to the store.
   3. Charlie | wants an ice cream cone.
   4. (My mom and dad) | took me shopping.
   5. His brown dog | wagged its tail.
   6. Main Street | is very busy.
   7. (The duck and the hen) | became friends.
   8. (The noisy girls and boys) | talked and talked during the movie.
E. 1. D
   2. A
   3. F
   4. E
   5. B
   6. C

F. 1. (I) ate a tasty hamburger.
   2. (Tony) rode a black horse.
   3. (Craig and I) hiked up the mountain.
   4. (The students) liked their teacher.
   5. (Daniel and Lily) studied together.
   6. (Calgary and Vancouver) are cities.
G. (Individual writing)

8 Sentences (2)

A. 1. plays
   2. are
   3. don't
   4. is
   5. was
   6. doesn't
   7. was
   8. is
   9. call
   10. has
   11. stick
   12. like
   13. enjoys
B. 1. prepares
   2. is
   3. thief
   4. ✔
   5. were
   6. and
   7. is
C. 1. The squirrel has eaten our cherries.
   2. The hunting dogs are well trained.
   3. The child was swimming in the pool.
   4. These rabbits always hide behind the bushes.
   5. That potato was taken from Grandpa's farm.
   6. This sheep has its wool shorn by the farmer.
D. 1. ✔
   2. ✔
   3.
   4.
   5. ✔
E. 1. Maple leaves change colour in fall.
   2. It is slippery to walk on the snow.
   3. The monkey is standing on the pole.
   4. We will complete the puzzle very soon.
F. 1. My computer is old but it still works.
   2. The beach is beautiful and it is easy to get to.
   3. I will join the party but I have to leave early.
   4. My brother is little and he needs to take an afternoon nap.
   5. We will watch the football game or we will go out for dinner.

9 Phrases and Clauses

A.
1. P
2. P
3. C
4. P
5. C
6. C
7. P
8. C

B.
1. on its mother's back
2. did his best
3. a helpful person
4. doing my homework
5. during the peak season

C.
1. our car broke down
2. I came last
3. we could finish the project
4. you go sailing
5. I'll have orange juice
6. it looks like new

D. (Underline these phrases.)
1. This boring movie
2. All of us ; the state-of-the-art cellular phone
3. our mouth-watering dishes
4. The appalling living conditions ; this area
5. a great sympathy ; the blind
6. that elegant white satin wedding gown
7. this tiny, fluffy creature
8. Hundreds of people ; free turkeys
9. The spectacular performance of the circus ; a lot of applause ; the audience

E.
1. at meal time
2. with a short tail
3. on the first page
4. at the beginning
5. of a frog

F. (Individual writing)

10 More on Phrases

A.
1. I wish I could (ride) a real horse.
2. Uncle Ben is (working) hard to build the fence.
3. They should have (tidied) up their rooms.
4. We will (have) a barbecue lunch tomorrow.
5. You should (keep) an eye on your luggage.
6. They will be (flying) to Vancouver tomorrow.

B.
1. is raining
2. will visit
3. were running
4. have visited
5. had tried
6. am watching

C.
1. B
2. L
3. L
4. L
5. B
6. L

D. (Individual writing)

E.
1. movie — terribly scary
2. baby koala — in its mother's pouch
3. book — with a hard cover
4. girl — with a big white bag
5. idea — totally outrageous
6. restaurant — near my house

F. (Individual writing)

G.
1. after school
2. for our team
3. high up
4. really hard
5. in the end

H. (Individual writing)

11 Punctuation

A.
1. The movie "Lord of the Rings" won many Oscars.
2. Have you read the book "Cat in the Hat"?
3. "Beauty and the Beast" is on at the Princess of Wales Theatre.
4. Mom always watches "The Naked Chef" for new recipes.
5. "Finding Nemo" is a popular movie.
6. Jamie asked, "Where's the key?"
7. We can call it "Project X".

B. (Individual writing)

C.
1. A
2. C
3. E
4. D
5. B

D.
1. Tim is a fast runner; he has won many medals.
2. Dad has a toothache; he doesn't want to eat.
3. This detective story is very interesting; I've read it many times.
4. Tomorrow is the last day of school; we need to clear our lockers.
5. My brother is crazy about SpongeBob; he has T-shirts with the character on them.

E.
1. P
2. C
3. C
4. P

F.
1. Jordan's
2. James's
3. musicians'

ISBN: 978-1-897457-04-7

G.

H. (Individual writing)

12 Prefixes and Suffixes

A. (Individual writing)
B. 1. (pre) caution
2. (re) dial
3. (mis) taken
4. (dis) honest
5. (un) believable
C. 1. ✔ dis
2.
3. ✔ re
4. ✔ mis
5.
6.
D. 1. pre
2. un
3. pre
4. dis
5. dis
6. mis
7. mis
8. un
9. re
E. (Circle these words.)
knowledgeable ; useful ; spineless ; usually ; harmless ; cautiously
F. 1. fashionable
2. tasteless
3. alertness
4. kindly
5. thoughtful

G. 1. useless
2. weakness
3. hopeful
4. affordable
5. hastily
6. fairness
H. (Individual writing)

13 Developing the Paragraph

A. 1. A
2. B
B. (Individual writing)
C. 1. 1 ; 2 ; 3
2. 2 ; 3 ; 1
3. 2 ; 1 ; 3
D. (Individual writing)

Progress Test 2

A. Hop | is very disappointed
Otherwise, I | would have saved you some
Scotch | is lying in the shade, picking his teeth
he | knows there are other things to eat in the forest
that | is not the only vegetable garden around
B. (Individual answers)
C. 1. help
2. arrive
3. says
4. is
5. has
6. decide
D. 1. N
2. ADJ
3. ADV
4. V
5. ADJ
6. N
7. P / ADJ
8. ADV
E. 1. he has not eaten all day
2. the friends look for another garden
3. they are very impressed
4. they are hungry, too
5. he hopes his friends will join him

F. 1. "It is a lovely day," says Flutter.
    2. Flutter believes that the song "Robin in the Rain" was about him.
    3. Since he likes gardens, Hop would probably enjoy the story "The Secret Garden".
    4. "This garden is very big!" says Buzzer. "In fact, I think it is the biggest garden I've ever seen."

G. 1. Hop isn't hungry anymore.
    2. Buzzer can't find more nectar even though he'd like to.
    3. These are Flutter's worms.
    4. Flutter and Buzzer are Hop's friends.
    5. Scotch doesn't know that there's a better garden.

H. 1. helpful
    2. Unlike
    3. redirects
    4. slowly
    5. dissatisfied

I. (Individual writing)

1 Seal Island

A. 1. feed   2. meat-eaters
3. hidden   4. trap
5. leaping   6. surprised
7. throwing

B. (Any 4)
1. safety ; shore ; squids ; schools ; small ; stalking ; seals ; sound ; surface ; September ; south ; surrounding ; shark ; spectacular ; swimming
2. main ; migrate ; makes ; months ; making ; move ; meal
3. cape ; crabs ; cooler ; carnivores ; can ; camouflaged ; capture
4. perfect ; peril ; predator ; prey

C. 1. B ; flesh-eaters / meat-eaters ; sharks (Suggested answer) ; seals (Suggested answer)
2. A ; vegetable-eaters / plant-eaters ; horses (Suggested answer) ; cows (Suggested answer)
3. C ; meat- and plant-eaters ; human beings (Suggested answer) ; dogs (Suggested answer)

D. (Individual writing)

2 More than Candy

A. 1. appealed   2. strategy
3. assorted   4. dispenser
5. conventions 6. originally

B. (Individual answers)

C. 1. E   2. G   3. J
4. I   5. B   6. D
7. A   8. F   9. C
10. H

D. (Individual answers)

E. (Individual answers)

F. (Individual design)

3 The Surprise Holiday

A. (Individual writing)

B. 1. C   2. E   3. D
4. H   5. F   6. G
7. B   8. A

C. Two Syllables : drowsy ; purchased ; suitcase ; question
Three Syllables : expressions ; disbelief ; vacation ; reactions
Four Syllables : everyone ; destination ; activities ; reality

D. 1. chil-dren   2. air-plane
3. par-ents   4. ho-tel
5. beau-tiful ; beauti-ful 6. hol-iday ; holi-day
7. di-rections ; direc-tions
8. hap-piness ; happi-ness

E. (Individual answers)

F. LATW ; SIYDEN ; RLODW
G. WALT DISNEY WORLD

4 Hear Ye...Hear Ye! (Part 1)

A.

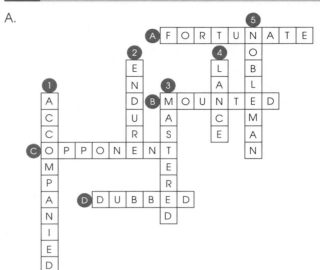

B. 1. please   2. greeting
3. teach   4. battlefield
5. cheer   6. dreamed
7. queen   8. brief
9. piece / peace 10. peace / piece
11. feelings   12. believed
13. leaving   14. needed
15. achieve

C. 1. friend ; Noblemen living in a castle
2. fighting ; About learning
3. servant ; For fighting
4. manners ; Skills a "page" had to learn
5. ceremony ; Traits needed to be a knight

D. "a" to "h" :
1. born   2. castle
3. ceremony   4. experiences
5. falcon   6. fighting
"i" to "p" :
1. knight   2. lady
3. lance   4. level
5. lord   6. manners
"q" to "z" :
1. riding   2. skills
3. stronger   4. taught
5. training   6. wrestling

E. (Individual writing)

5 Hear Ye...Hear Ye! (Part 2)

A. 1. E   2. D   3. G
4. I   5. C   6. A
7. J   8. B   9. H
10. F

ISBN: 978-1-897457-04-7

B. (Individual writing)
C. 1. today   2. slave
    3. pain   4. faith
    5. saying   6. shame
    7. stayed   8. plate
    9. praise   10. away
   11. training   12. bathed
   13. awaited   14. grateful
   15. displayed
D. 1. knight   2. knife
    3. knee   4. knead
    5. knot   6. knew
    7. knuckle   8. know
    9. knelt
Challenge
    knowledge
E. decide – demand :
    defend ; defeat ; deem ; deliver ; declare
    lord – loyal :
    loser ; loud ; lovely ; lower ; lost
    feast – festival :
    feather ; feed ; feat ; fellow ; feel
    tradition – trait :
    tragic ; trail ; training ; traipse
F. 1. Edward studied many years to become a knight.
    2. Would you like to live during the Middle Ages?
    3. Tomorrow Edward will be dubbed by Lord Henry.

6   The Case of the Disappearing Fish

A. Heron
B. 1. seafood   2. someone
    3. sunrise   4. backyard
    5. suitable   6. something
    7. waterfall   8. outside
Challenge
    neighbourhood
C.

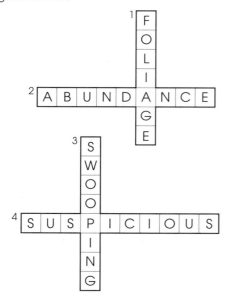

Crossword (top right):
- 5 ENVY (down)
- 6 CAPTIVITY (across)
- 7 LOCAL (down)
- 8 RECALLED (across)
- 9 SKIMMING (down)
- 10 DILIGENTLY (across)
- 11 CULPRIT (down)
- 12 SUITABLE (across)

D. (Individual writing)
E. • Suburbs near Rattray Marsh
    • José's beautiful backyard
    • Mysterious or puzzling mood
(Individual drawing)

7   Not a Typical Grandma

A. 1. C   2. B   3. C
    4. A   5. A   6. C
    7. B   8. A
B. B ; D ; E ; A ; C
C. "ou" words :
    1. sound   2. South
    3. outfits   4. mountain
    "ow" words :
    1. brown   2. down
D. 1. outside   2. flower
    3. crown   4. found
    5. flour   6. shout
    7. Mouse   8. cloudy
    9. Hound
Challenge
    allowance

E. (Individual writing)
F. (Individual answers)

Progress Test 1

A. 1. c. ; l.　　　　　2. tbsp. ; ml.
　 3. tsp. ; ml.　　　 4. c. ; ml.
　 5. c. ; ml.　　　　 6. c. ; ml.
　 7. tbsp. ; ml.　　 9. lg. ; pkg.
　 10. temp. ; F. ; C. ; min. ; dz. ; lg. ; dz. ; med.

B. Two Syllables :　 measure ; mixture ; flavour ; preheat
　 Three Syllables :　delicious ; tablespoon ; margarine ; appetite
　 Four Syllables :　 temperature ; appetizer ; decoration ; ingredient

C. 1. meat-eater　　　 2. jealous
　 3. interested　　　 4. neighbourhood
　 5. meetings　　　　 6. judge
　 7. mastery　　　　 8. clothing
　 9. delicious　　　 10. lived
　 11. cleanse　　　 12. forever
　 13. plenty　　　　 14. feed
　 15. diving　　　　 16. different

D. "a" to "h" :
　 1. apron　　　　　 2. chef
　 3. cupcake　　　　 4. dessert
　 5. eggs　　　　　 6. grill
　 "i" to "p" :
　 1. icing　　　　　 2. kitchen
　 3. muffins　　　　 4. nuts
　 5. oven　　　　　 6. pastry
　 "q" to "z" :
　 1. recipe　　　　 2. serving
　 3. snack　　　　　 4. sprinkles
　 5. tasty　　　　　 6. utensil

E. 1. do-nuts　　　　 2. rai-sins
　 3. car-amel ; cara-mel
　 4. cin-namon ; cinna-mon
　 5. choc-olate ; choco-late
　 6. dec-orate ; deco-rate
　 7. tem-perature ; temper-ature ; tempera-ture

F.

1.	dish	melon	dishwasher
2.	blue	scotch	blueberry
3.	clean	holder	cleanup
4.	water	spoon	watermelon
5.	butter	fruit	butterscotch
6.	tea	berry	teaspoon
7.	pot	washer	potholder
8.	grape	up	grapefruit

G. bagel – banana :
　 baker ; ball ; balance

chef – chop :
chill ; chestnut ; cherry ; chip ; chocolate
flaky – flour :
flatten ; flavour ; flipper ; flatware ; flapjack
special – spray :
spoon ; spice ; sponge ; split ; spend

H. 1. T　　　　 2. S　　　　 3. T
　 4. T　　　　 5. S　　　　 6. S

I. 1. B　　　　 2. C　　　　 3. A
　 4. C　　　　 5. B　　　　 6. A
　 7. B

J. 1. plate ; Silverware
　 2. cake ; Baking ingredients
　 3. candles ; Can be eaten
　 4. yogurt ; Things that are baked
　 5. brownies ; Types of cookies

K. long "a" sound :
　 spray ; grain ; tasty (taste) ; tray ; scale
　 long "e" sound :
　 grease ; piece ; cream ; yield ; peel
　 "ow" sound :
　 flour ; paper towel ; ground ; brown ; pound

8 Being the Eldest

A. (Individual writing)
B. 1. secluded　　　 2. quantities
　 3. siblings　　　 4. role model
C. 4 ; 5 ; 3
D. 1. advantage　　 2. young
　 3. interest　　　 4. total
　 5. irritate　　　 6. regard
　 7. practise　　　 8. quantity
E.　 Evan loved to climb in the attic where he had a secret hideaway. He kept his favourite toys and books up there. Evan also stored Christmas presents for his family in the attic. He made sure nobody followed him when he escaped to his hideout.

9 The Mud Puppy and Friends

A. 1. D　　　　 2. H　　　　 3. E
　 4. B　　　　 5. G　　　　 6. F
　 7. A　　　　 8. C

B. (Individual writing)
C. 1. triathlete ; an athlete that does three sports
　 2. misread ; understood wrongly
　 3. uncertain ; not sure
　 4. dismounted ; got off
　 5. prejudged ; judged before something really happened
D. 1. The race car ; a bolt of lightning
　 2. The cyclist ; sizzling bacon

3. His mouth ; desert sand
E. (Individual answers)

10 A Rebus Invitation

A. Dear Stacey,
   You are invited to my birthday party on Sunday, July 1st. It starts at 2 o'clock and ends at 5 o'clock. We will meet at the Wheeler Horse Farm on Queen Street. Lunch will be hot dogs, french fries, and cupcakes. Please bring sunscreen and bug spray.

   Your friend,
   Shelley

B. (Individual answers)
C. (Individual answers)
D. (Individual writing)
E.
1. happiness	2. baker
3. dancing	4. thankless
5. excitable	6. wishful
7. decorator	8. fearless
9. usually	10. teachable
11. climbed	12. flavourful

11 A Sporty Gal

A. (Suggested answers)
1. However	2. Finally
3. before	4. after
5. As a result	6. As soon as

B. (Individual writing)
C. 1. basketball
   2. The Olympic Games
D. (Suggested answers)
   score : store ; restore ; more ; door ; roar
   kick : tick ; click ; quick ; sick ; trick
   speed : bleed ; deed ; weed ; seed ; read
   goal : roll ; sole ; role ; coal ; pole
E. (Individual writing)

12 Cornfield Today, Volcano Tomorrow

A.
1. phone	2. afloat
3. overflow	4. soul
5. throw	6. though
7. bulldoze	8. close
9. grown	10. shadow
11. raincoat	12. dough

B.
1. pianist	2. machinist
3. scientist	4. geologist
5. violinist	6. florist
7. dentist	8. pharmacist

C. 1. rumbling   2. crack
   3. whistling

D.
1. old windows on a windy day	splash
2. eating potato chips	clang
3. eating spaghetti	crunch
4. jumping in a pool	bark
5. washing dishes	slurp
6. sound of a dog	rattle

E. (Individual writing)
F. 1. B   2. A
   3. A   4. B
G. (Individual writing)

13 Nature's Fireworks

A. (Definitions : Individual answers)
   1. causing fear for being strange
   2. send out
   3. in or of times long ago
   4. bright and strong, producing a sharp sensation on the eyes
   5. very small pieces
   6. something that causes wonder and admiration
   7. sign that something is going to happen in the future
B. (Individual writing)
C. (Individual writing)
D. A ; B ; D
E. (Individual writing)

14 A Pet's Tale

A. C ; E ; A ; F ; D ; B
Challenge
   A dog
B. (Individual answers)
   (Individual writing)
C. (Individual answers)
Challenge
   (Individual writing)
D.
1. sail	2. deer
3. plane	4. heel
5. bear	6. rain
7. pear	8. flower

E. 1. Their ; there   2. rode ; road
   3. hole ; whole   4. hare ; hair
   5. threw ; through   6. write ; right

15 Camp Wannastay

A. 1. C   2. E
   3. F   4. A
   5. B   6. D

   ISBN: 978-1-897457-04-7

B. 1. The concerned counsellor took a thorough look around for poison ivy.
2. We heard a startling noise and ran swiftly to our cabin.
3. Although my time at camp was brief, I had an enjoyable experience.
4. They gave generous portions of dessert and it was always scrumptious.
5. By the end of our lengthy hiking excursion, I felt extremely weary.

C. (Individual writing)

D. 1. bought 2. caught
3. fought 4. brought
5. thought 6. taught

E. 1. rough 2. laugh
3. cough 4. trough
5. tough

F. (Individual design)

Progress Test 2

A. 1. company 2. best
3. clubhouse 4. groovy
5. backyard 6. jokes
7. relationship 8. strong

B. 1. unsuccessful 2. frightful
3. disappear 4. endless
5. wonderful 6. performance
7. friendliest 8. suddenly
9. unbelievable

C. 1. wonderful 2. performer
3. novelist 4. thoughtless
5. laughable 6. carefully
7. sailor 8. happiness

D. 1. bored 2. cent
3. there 4. ware / wear
5. bean 6. new
7. threw 8. eye
9. ours 10. eight

E. Sight : bright ; blurry ; shiny
Sound : crackling ; whistling ; swishing
Smell : rotten ; skunky ; fruity
Taste : spicy ; bitter ; tangy
Touch : silky ; squishy ; fuzzy

F. 1. We practised our dance moves until we mastered them.
2. Madison and Nicole attended each other's parties.
3. We studied many school subjects together.

G. Madison and Nicole keep themselves busy when they're together. First, they disappear into the clubhouse for a game of cards. Then, they check out the fridge for snacks and drinks. After their snack break, Nicole and Madison listen to music. Before they head out to the backyard, they play a board game

or two. Finally, they settle in for secrets on the hammock.

H. 1. swift ; fast 2. many ; numerous
3. start ; initiate 4. oldest ; eldest
5. pester ; annoy 6. short ; brief
7. victory ; win 8. ruckus ; noisy
9. vivid ; bright 10. marvel ; wonder

I. 1. frightened 2. excited
3. sad 4. happy
5. angry / frustrated

J. 1. chirping 2. boom
3. popped 4. clanged
5. buzzed

K. 1. mis ; understand something wrongly
2. dis ; oppose
3. mid ; middle of the night
4. tri ; three colours
5. pre ; plan in advance
6. un ; open

L. 1. E 2. F
3. G 4. A
5. C 6. B
7. D

M. 1. C 2. C
3. C ; D ; A ; B

1. I HAVE HAD GREAT FUN HERE AND I WILL VISIT YOU AGAIN NEXT YEAR.

2.

3.

4.

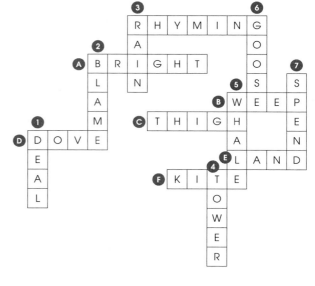

Crossword:

3 R H Y M I N G	6 G
2 R A	O
A B R I G H T	O
B L A N	S 7 S
A M	5 S
1 M	B W E E P	P
D D O V E	C T H I G H A	E
E	A	N
A	E L A N D	
L	4 K I T E	
F K I T E	O	
	W	
	E	
	R	

5.

ISBN: 978-1-897457-04-7

6.

I	D	j	f	n	D	A	u	g	u	s	t
F	e	O	A	J	h	e	O	l	e	i	d
j	c	b	c	M	a	r	c	h	k	u	N
S	e	J	J	t	N	n	c	S	F	o	h
A	m	g	u	D	o	a	u	M	e	J	k
h	b	M	I	n	v	b	s	a	b	t	a
m	e	o	y	F	e	N	e	y	r	s	y
s	r	e	m	V	m	b	w	r	u	y	n
O	b	J	i	O	b	e	M	g	a	z	k
n	S	e	p	t	e	m	b	e	r	x	p
j	a	k	A	p	r	i	l	c	y	d	r
c	e	o	M	g	D	f	d	i	l	m	e

7.

1. STEAL
2. THINK
3. SCARCE
4. SEAT
5. CHIEF
6. FLIGHT
7. GRAIN
8. EXIST / EXITS
9. SWING
10. TUBE
11. REPLY
12. BOAT

8.

rose → rise → rice → dice

near → neat → beat → bean

9.

E L V E S O X E N

H E R O E S C ...
(crossword grid with ELVES, OXEN, HEROES, etc.)

10.

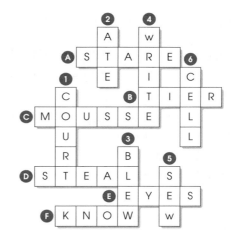

A. S T A R E
B. T I E R
C. M O U S S E
D. S T E A L S
E. E Y E S
F. K N O W

11.

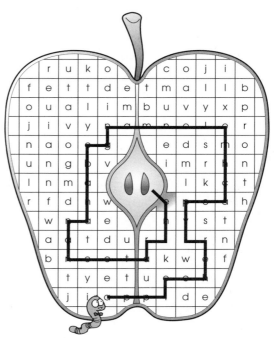

r	u	k	o		c	o	j	i
f	e	t	t	d	e	t	m	a	l	l	b
o	u	a	l	i	m	b	u	v	y	x	p
j	i	v	y	y	p	a	m	p	e	l	e	r
n	a	o	e	g		e	d	s	m	o
u	n	g	o	v		i	m	r	i	n
l	n	m	a		l	k	e	t
r	f	d	n	w		u	s	t	h
w	h	d	e			i	s	t
a	d	t	d	u	r		n
b	o	o	t	k	w	e	f
t	y	e	t	u	o	
j	i	a	p	p		d	e

ISBN: 978-1-897457-04-7

12.

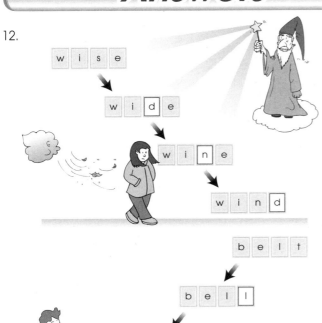

wise → wide → wine → wind

belt → bell → well → wall

15.

road → roar → rear → near → bear → bead → head → heat

13. 1. EAR ; PEA ; PAR ; PER ; ERA
   2. EEL ; LET ; BET ; BEE ; TEE
   3. GEM ; TEN ; MEN ; NET ; MET
   4. HIS ; HIT ; SIT ; ITS ; SIR

14. 1. Kangaroo   2. alien
    3. statue   4. hammer
    5. fork   6. turtle
    7. toboggan   8. envelope
    9. video game

16.

c	e	g	y	p	k	d	c	i	m	f	g
f	j	p	m	u	s	h	r	o	o	m	o
a	a	d	o	m	b	g	c	h	r	b	k
i	n	r	q	p	r	r	m	a	w	n	e
l	t	u	t	k	o	n	i	o	n	i	g
a	o	d	r	i	c	j	o	t	r	n	g
c	m	s	n	n	c	p	y	b	a	k	p
e	a	j	c	g	o	h	v	x	t	e	l
l	t	r	t	b	l	u	o	z	b	h	a
e	o	i	r	d	i	l	s	k	e	q	n
r	h	e	p	o	t	a	t	o	e	i	t
y	b	p	j	s	t	m	u	s	t	e	b

ISBN: 978-1-897457-04-7